THE BIRDS SANG EULOGIES

A MEMOIR

BY MIRLA GECLEWICZ RAZ

Copyright © 2019

Library of Congress Control Number: 2019904426

ISBN: 978-0-9635426-6-3

Cover page photograph by Henryk Ross
Resident (Gedalia Geclewicz) tagged for deportation to Auschwitz, Lodz Ghetto, 1942-1944
Gift from Archive of Modern Conflict, 2007
Cover photo © Art Gallery of Ontario

In memory of my beloved parents, Anna and Daniel Geslewitz, and my grandparents, aunts, uncles and cousins who perished in the Holocaust.

"But we Jews oppose the Nazis' determination to destroy and annihilate the Jewish people with our own determination to remember, with our precise and intransigent Jewish memory."

"...his conscience as a Christian was able to accommodate the Nazi regime's anti-Semitism."

Beate Klarsfeld, Hunting the Truth: Memoirs of Beate and Serge Klarfled, 2015

Contents

My Story

I am a member of a group called the Second Generation. Each person of this community is a member for their own personal reasons. Some members derive comfort from sharing stories of their lives with other children of survivors. The survivors believed only other survivors could truly understand what they went through. There are children of survivors who feel that way about their lives as survivors' children. Other members wish to educate young people about the Holocaust. They feel the obligation to carry on the legacies of their parents so that the Holocaust is never forgotten or denied once all the survivors are gone. Each of us has dealt with our parents' traumas in our own way.

It is hard to explain what it means to be a child of Holocaust survivors and to have been cut off from nearly the entirety of one's roots. What would it have been like to have grandparents and a large extended family? What were my grandparents and my aunts and uncles like? Who do I look like? I grilled my parents on the physical appearances of their parents and brother and sisters. You have my mother's hair, my father said. And she was about your height. But, I will never really know because neither my mother nor father has a single picture of their lives before the Holocaust.

I think back to my visit to Auschwitz. I remember looking around at the pictures of European Jews. I remember seeing the men, women and children who had made up the fabric of European Jewish life for centuries. Their lives had been hard. They lived through pogroms. They faced discrimination by the Christians who surrounded them. The governments, whose job it was to protect them, did not because, in most cases, government officials were complicit in the discrimination and pogroms against their Jewish citizens. Life was not easy for my people. And then came Germany with its Hitler and Nazis. Who knows how many future doctors, scientists, and teachers were murdered, children who would have one day grown up to help mankind.

The scars resulting from the traumas of the Holocaust survivors never went away. There is life to their memories—their mothers, fathers, sisters, brothers, cousins, aunts, uncles and friends and neighbors. Their fond memories alongside the horrific. The normal alongside the abnormal. For the survivors one does not have one without the other. The survivors resurrected their lives as best as they could. Their lives were a picture of normalcy. They had children who thrived and, for the most part, became successful citizens of their parents' adopted countries. What could be more normal than that? Yet.... my father-in-law used to say that one cannot have survived the Holocaust and be normal afterward. My father fought against this idea, believing that the survivors remained normal despite the Holocaust. Who is right?

To understand what happened I have to suspend my beliefs in what is normal. To understand what happened I have to suspend my beliefs in what is sane. I have to let go and believe the stories because they are not fiction. Even so, I will find it impossible to understand that world and time. But I must try to understand. An impossible task because only those who lived through it can understand the story of human degradation at its absolute worst. If I deny the story or lighten it, I will never understand the horrendous acts our species can commit, nor will I ever understand the expanse of human resilience and existence. Why people fight to live. How they succeed. So, I take myself out of my comfort bubble and believe.

I am the beneficiary of one of the greatest tragedies the world has ever known. My luck is firmly rooted in the cataclysmic bad luck of European Jewry. Were it not for this colossal tragedy, my parents most definitely would not have met, married nor had my sisters or me. That I am an heir of this epic tragedy makes me keenly aware that my parents, their parents, sisters, brothers, cousins, nephew, friends, neighbors and millions more Jews suffered before it could happen. My good fortune, being born after WWII, did not come without a price. I never had the opportunity to meet my grandparents, aunts, uncles, a first cousin and other extended family members. One maternal aunt and one paternal uncle survived out of a total of twelve. Other than a prewar picture of my paternal great aunt, I have not one picture of any family member taken before the war. Yet, I was fortunate that a little piece of my European family survived. There are families that were entirely obliterated or only one family member is the sole survivor.

In most ways, my life growing up in the United States was typical of children born to immigrant parents. My parents felt most comfortable around other European survivors who had shared similar lives in Europe. Our food was similar, they could converse in Yiddish or Polish, and their values remained European.

As the first born, I was immersed in two foreign languages from birth, so learning other languages was easy for me. Growing up, my American life had little to do with my parents' experiences, which is exactly how my parents wanted it. They wanted my sisters and me to only know the good in life and to live in a country where we could grow up Jewish and safe. My parents took full advantage of what America offered. They would work hard so their children would have better lives. Their children would go to college. Everything was possible in America.

Sometimes the Old World conflicted with the American model. The big challenges for me began when I became a teenager. My parents found it difficult to adapt to the freedoms of American teenagers. Everything became a fight. Then again, the teenage years are fraught with parents and teens having to put up with one another. But there were battles my friends did not have with their parents. For one, having them agree to allow me to go away to college was preceded by huge wars. They finally gave in but insisted on no more than an hour driving radius. My father had a timeline that coincided with European ideas of what young women should do. The day I finished college was the day my father decided that I had to find a husband to take care of me. That was his timeline. Get a college education, get married and have children. He pressed me to go into teaching since I would have the same hours as my future children. Yet, at other times, he was more forward thinking. He often encouraged me to become a doctor or lawyer.

Did being the child of parents who had been in the Holocaust have its emotional impact on me? I find it hard to watch movies or read about it. I tend to have little patience with people, especially Jews, who make innocent but ignorant comments about the Holocaust. I was talking with a Jewish friend whose mother was born in America and whose father was from Canada. I told her that I wanted to talk to her mother about what she knew about European Jewry during the Holocaust years. My friend asked me why I did not ask my parents when they were alive. I told her that they did not arrive until 1950. She said, "Oh, I thought they came in the 40s." I immediately lashed out at her and said, "There were hardly any Jews who could get here in the 40s!" Her reply was, "Well, some Jews did." I didn't tell her what my parents had said about the ignorance of American Jews and their uncaring attitudes vis a vis the survivors. I told her that she needed to become better informed about the Holocaust. She accused me of talking down to her.

I am also thinned skinned when I am in the presence of someone who denies aspects of what occurred during the Holocaust. When I was in my 20s and living in Los Angeles. I was working in the inner city and carpooled to work with two fellow teachers. The driver was Jewish and the other passenger was not. One day the other passenger said that there is no proof that 6 million Jews were murdered. I laid into him. "What do you mean there's no proof? You need to educate yourself about the Holocaust instead of perpetuating lies! You sound like a neo

Nazi," I shouted unable to control my anger. During lunch, a couple of teachers approached me and told me that they had heard what happened. They congratulated me for confronting him. Then there was the Nazi demonstration in front the Federal Building in Los Angeles. My friend from Palo Alto had come to visit and we were driving to the mall to shop for her wedding dress. As we passed the Federal Building, I noticed that there were a lot of signs and people. I asked Susan what was going on. She told me, "A bunch of Nazis are demonstrating." Furious, I immediately made a sharp right into the parking lot. I marched out of the car. My baffled friend followed me. There were Neo-Nazis carrying placards, policemen keeping the peace and a small group of about 20 people listening to someone on a platform. I stood in the middle of the crowd and immediately began hurling a litany of curses at the speaker. I noticed that he had acne scars so I called him a pocked faced creep. I have a good set of lungs and was making myself heard. When I finished hurling insults at him, I passed by each tough looking placard bearer (they were dressed in biker black with all sorts of metal hanging from them) and repeated my litany of curse words. Then I looked at my friend, who at this point looked petrified beyond belief, and said, "Okay. I'm done. Now we can go."

With my parents, I would watch movies made about the Holocaust: "Sophie's Choice," "Escape from Sobibor," "Europa Europa," "Schindler's List," to name a few. I would ask my parents if the movie depicted what they experienced. Their answer was that not one movie came close. They used to say the movies were Hollywood's whitewashed versions. My father said that "Life Is Beautiful" was a ridiculous fairytale and a stupid movie. My mother said that "Schindler's List" was the most accurate of the movies, but still a far cry from the reality she experienced. The takeaway fact is that there is no one who will ever understand the Holocaust, unless he or she survived it. How can we understand the experience of European Jewry during World War II if we are not hungry for days, months and then years? Can we understand daily fear and torment if we are not witnessing fellow citizens falling dead on the street, if we do not witness murder daily? Can we grasp what it means to not wash for months, if we shower daily? Can we understand the smell of dead bodies rotting alongside thousands of unwashed, lice infested bodies sleeping? How can we understand the Holocaust if our senses have not been bombarded by daily murder and humiliation, constant gut-wrenching hunger, the smell of filth and dead rotting bodies, the constant feel of lice sucking at one's skin, the moans, groans and screams of people being tortured, witnessing family members murdered one-by-one? How does a person feel knowing that there is no one in the world who cares enough to come to one's rescue?

Everybody rises as the survivors slowly and gingerly make their way into the hall and down the aisle to be seated up front. Most are in their 90s. They are old and fragile. The majority of the survivors have passed. Soon they will be gone too, these special people. My eyes well up with tears. They are the Jews who have borne witness to the atrocities humans can foist on other humans. They are an unbelievable generation who managed to lay down new roots, rebuild their lives and give birth to new generations. They are a special people. I cry for their passing and for leaving us alone to try to keep the Holocaust relevant to our children and their children and their children ..... .

Trip Back East

My husband and I are traveling back east for a wedding in New York City in May. We add a two-day stop in New Orleans, since I have never been there.

On March 29, 2017, my husband shows me an article in the Wall Street Journal, "'Memory Unearthed: The Lodz Ghetto Photographs of Henryk Ross' Review: Photos From Inside The Holocaust." Henryk Ross was a Jewish photographer before the war. When the war broke out, the Germans confiscated his equipment. After the Germans sealed off the ghetto from the rest of Lodz, they decided to make propaganda pictures of ghetto life. They gave Henryk a camera. He became one of two Nazi sanctioned photographers whose job was to produce propaganda photographs for the German Department of Statistics. My husband points out that the exhibit will be at the Fine Arts Museum of Boston until July 2017. He suggests that we add Boston to our itinerary. I waver because I have Ross's 2004 publication. My father had criticized the 2004 publication because the pictures depicted the "privileged" more than the real-life pictures of the ghetto. I read the Wall Street Journal article. It emphasizes that many of the pictures have never before been published. Ross had buried them before the liquidation of the ghetto. I look at the pictures in the paper. There are a couple of photos that are not in the 2004 book. I figure that we can also visit my cousin Ronn's brewery, in Somerville, outside of Boston, so that the trip will not be a complete waste if the photographs disappoint.

May 2017

Our first stop was New Orleans. It is a lovely city, easy to navigate and with great food. On our last day, having seen what we thought were the highlights of the city, my husband and I pondered what else to do. I suggested the WWII museum. My husband, who is not a fan of museums, hemmed and hawed but agreed. The minute I stepped into the lobby and saw the WWII aircraft dangling from the enormously high ceiling, I knew we had made a good choice by coming. We wandered around this interactive museum for four hours. Since my knowledge of the Pacific front was sparse, I found this part of the museum to be a learning experience. The horrors that the Japanese imposed on their Asian neighbors and prisoners of war could have rivaled the Germans. Like the Germans, the Japanese were brutal and heartless captors. However, the Japanese did not attempt to annihilate, from the face of the earth, entire groups of people.

After our trip to New York, Zohar, my cousin Helen and I took the train to Boston. Helen and I are related through our fathers; her father and my dad were first cousins. Her father, Hirsch (Hirsch in Yiddish, Henyk in Polish) Zyngier, survived the Lodz Ghetto, was shipped to Auschwitz and two weeks later was sent to the Flossenburg concentration camp.

The exhibit was in a miniscule part of the huge and impressive Boston Fine Arts Museum. We walked through numerous galleries to get to it. After stepping into the doors of the exhibit, we watched a film of Henryk and his wife, Stephania. They were talking about the pictures and life in the ghetto. Although Henryk took the pictures, his wife was an important collaborator. They worked together to photograph ghetto life as it really was, not just the propaganda photographs the Germans wanted the world to see and believe. In the film, Stephania talked about the horrors of daily ghetto life and the suffering of its inhabitants. She said that starvation caused some people to become skeletal while others swelled, especially their legs and feet. They, and others who assisted them, took the photographs at great risk to themselves. The Nazis, had they suspected what Henryk and Stephania were doing, would have murdered them on the spot. Just before they were shipped out to Auschwitz, during the final liquidation of the ghetto, they buried the photographs in metal canisters. Neither had expected to survive but hoped that the buried photographs would eventually be found. As fortune would have it, the couple and their photographs survived. Henryk said that after the war he never took another picture.

I noted that many of the photographs were the same as in Henryk Ross's 2004 book where the "privileged" looked healthy, clean and well fed. They were the Jews who administered the ghetto, the policemen, the firefighters and their families. In the propaganda photos, the Jews looked like they were enjoying life in the ghetto. In reality, the photos belied the real ghetto life of suffering and anguish. Yet, I could not blame the Jews who were the "privileged." Each Jew was on his and her own to survive in any way possible. If they got a bit more food than most of the ghetto population, they were the lucky ones.

I walked around the gallery and inside of me was the hope that I would see a picture of my father or uncle in one of the groups of factory workers. I examined each picture looking for photos of woodworkers but did not find any. I was disappointed but not surprised. The ghetto was home to thousands. The chances of my father or uncle being in one of the photos was slim. Then, my eyes locked onto one blurry photograph of a young man (book cover photo). I stopped in my tracks and stared at the picture. As this young man is being herded with other ghetto Jews, he is looking to his right, so most of what is visible is his left profile. The unnamed young man looks to be about 20 years old. I examined the picture and said to myself, that is my father! The picture caption identified the photo as being taken during a deportation sometime between 1942-1944. My father was deported in August 1944 at the age of 20.

I immediately texted my nephew, Lee, and asked him to send me a picture of my father taken after the war when he was in Germany. He sent a picture right back. The cheek and jaw lines, the chins and lower lips are the same. The hairline above the ears is too. The young man has large protruding ears. Surprisingly, the ears are also similar. My father's ears were large and protruded. The hands of my father and the young man look identical. Both young men are good looking.

When I arrived home, I set out to find out how to determine if the young man is my father. I examined the photos of my dad in Germany with a magnifying glass. I read about digital analysis of facial features. Many experts believe that human analysis is more accurate for a number of reasons. I called the United States Holocaust Memorial Museum. The researcher I spoke with was not able to refer me to an expert in facial feature identification but informed me that the ear lobe attachments are used to identify people, since they do not change over time. I examined my father's ear lobe attachment and that of the young man. The young man's is a bit blurry and obscured by something white behind it. I called Scottsdale Police Department and spoke to one of their detectives. She told me that they do not have the need for facial feature identification. That is generally something the FBI does. The person I spoke with at the FBI could not help me since only agents are involved in the process. No, he could not connect me to an agent. I left my name and phone number with him in case he happened to hear about an agent who could assist me. Perhaps the agent could contact me. I never heard from anyone. In the meantime, my husband and I examined the images

9

under different magnifying glasses. I noticed that the pattern of the inside of the outer ear of the young man looks the same as my father's.

After some Google research, my husband found a specialist in facial analysis. I sent her the photos and she wrote back, "I do agree that it looks like it could possibly be your father. …I can't measure his ear properly because of the blurriness. Also, ears are the very best identifiers when they are visible, and the one visible in the picture is too blurry to analyze."

I contacted the Art Gallery of Ontario, in Toronto, which houses the photographs. I spoke with Maia Sutnik, the curator of Memories Unearthed. She said that since the exhibition had been displayed, a few people had identified or claimed to know some of the individuals in the photographs. I told her about my dad and she asked me to send her digital photos of my father. I sent her the pictures. She wrote back, "…I would say from a 'face recognition' perspective, the photographs taken by Henryk Ross may likely be of your father…. the photograph was taken quickly and the focus is not precise. However, more than the face, I am looking at the side hairline and the ear – these are features convincing to my eye." I knew it! The young man has to be my father. I am 99 percent certain that he is my father. Sutnik agreed. The photo, at all upcoming exhibits, will be identified as Gedalia Geclewicz taken August 27, 1944 on the way to the train that will take him to Auschwitz.

At home, I stare at the picture of the young man. His face speaks volumes about a defining moment in his young life: fear, concern, worry, confusion. Is he ready to cry? In the ghetto, rumor had it that Jews were being gassed, burned, buried alive. As bad as it was in the ghetto, this young man's face shows that he fears that where he is headed will be worse. Who is he turning his head to look at? I look at the picture with a knot of dread in my stomach. I know that what he will endure will nearly take his life. I look at this young handsome man. I know what fate awaits him within 24 hours and for the next nine months. He will be transported to Auschwitz, the real hell on earth, worse than he can ever imagine. He will be separated from his mother, two sisters and nephew. His mother, sister and nephew will be gassed and cremated within hours of their arrival at Auschwitz. He will see their smoke rise from the chimneys. His other sister will die on the death march out of Bergen-Belsen a few months before liberation. He will witness the death of two of his brothers in the camps, the oldest from an agonizing death five weeks before liberation. This young man will nearly die from starvation and severe diarrhea. My emotions overcome me and tears fill my eyes.

The Tree Limbs

Author's note: My parents' words are italicized. My and Keren's questions, comments, and clarifications are unitalicized. There are times when my father refers to me as Marilyn. My legal name is Mirla. However, an American cousin of my father said to call me Marilyn instead. Family and friends from childhood know me as Marilyn.

Mirla (daughter)

I am decluttering my older daughter's old bedroom when I come upon a coil bound book titled "The Third Generation." Keren wrote it as her senior thesis in college. I had forgotten that she had written about her grandfather's life during the Holocaust. Curious, I start reading it. I am drawn in. She moves me with her attempts to fashion the story of her grandfather's experiences. I had not known that she harbored such strong emotions. She writes about her difficulties understanding that period in her grandfather's life. As I read, I notice her approach-avoidance attempt to understand. She wants to understand but she never will. She does not want to truly understand because it may open a Pandora's box of unknown emotions that may be difficult to control. It is scary for her. I know that so well because I am in the same place. We understand the words of my father but stand on the other side of an opaque wall, looking in but unable to fathom what happened. Yet, years after they lived through that horrific time, Holocaust survivors admit that they have a hard time fathoming what happened to them and their families.

Keren (granddaughter)

I needed to get my grandfather's story straight. I had this project and after Lodz and Auschwitz I could not figure out where he had been in Germany. I sat down with him and unfolded a table-sized map.

Here, you know what, I tell you, your mom has a folder with my cards from Germany. Marilyn! Where is that folder?

My mom had been watching television in the family room, but she got up at my grandpa's request. She ducked into her office and then came out with a thick file folder full of yellow and yellowing papers. She set the papers down before my grandfather and then sat down to join us.

You see here, this is…no, this is not what I was looking for.

As he flipped through paper after paper, searching for his German labor camp identification card and explaining anything else he came across, one single sheet

13

ripped out of a yellow legal pad caught my eye. I opened it up and found the family tree. My great grandparents sat at the top. Beneath them were seven children. Except for two branches, the tree was stunted. My great uncle and grandpa's families sprouted across the page, taking up the spaces left blank by Meyer, Haya, Hersch, Shmiel and Leah. To think how big my family would be if there had been no Nazis.

My Father

Mirla

My father died on February 19, 2011. He was a loving, affectionate and generous man with a big heart. He approached life in what he would say was a common sense and practical way. Either something made sense to him or it did not. He was honest in his personal and business dealings. He was a hard worker and would do anything for his family. We were his life. However, he did have a dark side. He was prone to unpredictable mood swings and had a temper that he detonated not infrequently. He never showed this side to anyone else. To others he was sociable, talkative, a joker, kind and fun.

My father died because he chose to do so. He passed away two months after my mother. From the age of 80, he suffered physically. He had prostate cancer for which he received drug treatments. For six years after the treatments began, he complained of excruciating pain in his knees. No physical reason could be found and nothing fully stopped the pain; medications only eased it. When he was 81, he was diagnosed with multiple myeloma. Although it was controlled, he needed monthly chemotherapy infusions to keep it at bay. When my mom passed, I think he decided that he had had enough of the pain. I do not think he wanted to go on living without her. A few days before my mother died, he had been hospitalized to have a stent placed to help reduce the pain in his knees. When he left for the hospital, my mother had been mobile. When he returned home, my mother was in bed and unresponsive.

My mother was the one person in the world who put up with him 24/7. She was his audience, his ear, and his life-long supporter. He knew that there was no one who would do for him what she did. She stood between him and the hassles of his children and the outside world. When Mom died, my dad was left to deal with life's hassles on his own. So, he decided to die. Watching my dad's once sturdy body waste away was made more poignantly agonizing because he began to look like his description of himself right after the war, just like the photographs of concentration camp victims I had seen.

The Joy of a Small Discovery

Mirla

My dad was about 12 or 13 years old and walking home on a Friday afternoon, when he saw a leather belt lying on the ground. For a couple of years, he had been longing for a belt. A belt would symbolize his transition from boyhood to manhood. His parents could not afford to buy him one and although he worked in his dad's shop, he didn't earn money because all monies went to the family. Now on this lucky day, he had found a belt! He no longer needed to wear suspenders. Those were only for children. He could now wear a belt just like his dad and older brothers did.

The belt is 43 ½ inches long with a patterned metal buckle. It has four neatly made holes spaced within the first seven-and-a-half inches. It is hard to tell which of the holes my father used when he found the belt. This belt is the only remnant my father was able to save from his former life in Poland. The leather belt is a witness to the years between 1939 and 1945, the years that my dad was imprisoned and starved by the Nazis. Each notch on the belt is the eyewitness to my dad's worsening condition.

Keren

My grandfather skipped home with his new prize. He was 13 and he could lose the childish suspenders. More eager than ever to start Shabbat, he got to work right away helping his mother clean the house and set the table. His family would welcome the Sabbath bride in four hours. Everything had to sparkle. My grandfather and his sister Leah scrubbed the dining room floor and dusted all the furniture. They set out the best tablecloth and laid upon it the best dishes. Then they got dressed. At the far end of the closet, he reached for the white shirt with the starched collar he only wore once a week. Then he slipped on his best black pants, followed by his shiny black shoes. He tucked in his shirt to hide the small stain at the bottom. Last, he proudly and eagerly put his new belt through the loops.

Family members began to fill the room, as the sky outside grew darker. Voices filled the air as hugs and kisses were passed around. Mirla (my grandfather's mother, after whom my mother is named) silenced everyone as she lit the Shabbat candles. Itzhak, my great grandfather, held up the Kiddush cup and said the bracha. Taking a sip of wine from the Kiddush cup he passed the silver cup to his wife. This is the way it should always be, my grandfather thought as he looked around him. Always.

It is the most memorable memory, the memory of happiness that I can remember like yesterday. Every Friday, the whole family got together for family dinner. Till the Germans came in that was the most memorable dinner. When the Germans came in, everything was turned upside down. Everything was topsy turvy. There were no more Friday dinners. There was no food.

Danny's Story

Parents and Siblings of Daniel Geslewitz

Murdered by the Nazis

Survived the Holocaust

Itzhak Lazer Geclewicz 1885-1943

Mirla Weitz 1888-1944

Meyer Geclewicz 1910-1945

Hirsh Geclewicz 1911-1941

Haya Geclewicz Sonnabend 1914?-1944

Leon Geslewitz 1916-2004

Shmiel (Shmuel) Geclewicz 1919-1944

Laya (Leah) Geclewicz 1922-1945

Daniel (Gedalia) Geslewitz 1924-2011

Eva Pasternak 1919-1987?

Tovia Sonnabend ??-??

Yossel Sonnabend 1940-1944

18

The Family

*I was born Gedalia Geclewicz on August 14, 1924 to Mirla Weitz Geclewicz (born 1888)
and Itzhak Lezer Geclewicz (born 1885). I was the youngest of seven children. My brother
Meyer was born in 1910, Hirsh was born in 1912, Haya was born in 1914, Leyva [Leon]
was born in 1916, Schmiel was born in 1919, and Leah was born in 1922. We lived in Lodz,
Poland. My father was hard working and a very honest man. He was over 6 feet tall. He was
called the, Hoi'echa Itzik or Tall Itzik. My mother was a very devoted wife and mother. My
mother was about 5 feet 3 inches and had dark curly hair. Just like yours* (referring to me).
*My brother Meyer was a handsome guy, very handsome. He was about 6 feet tall. Leon was the
shortest. Leon was blond, the only blond in the family. Hirsh was about my size, 5 foot 9 inches.
My sisters had curly hair and were taller than my mother. The whole family was good-looking.
I survived the Holocaust with only my brother Leon. Everyone else was murdered by the
Germans.*

*My sister Haya married Toivia Sonnenbend in 1938. They had a son, Yossel, who was
born in 1940 in Lodz. Meyer married Eva Pasternak in 1940 at the beginning of the ghetto.
Leon married Rushka, whose family name I don't remember.*

*My father was a cabinetmaker and my mother was a homemaker. My father had his own
business where all his sons worked with him. My father's shop was on the first floor of our
building, the shtebel* (small one-room synagogue) *was on the 2nd floor, and we lived on the
3rd floor. My mom worked hard. She prepared meals and worked hard to keep the household
running. Major laundering was done every four weeks. Laundry had to be boiled, hung to dry,
folded. It was whole operation. She had to walk to the market at Baluti Rynek and carry all
groceries. She baked challah, made noodles, prepared fish. It was a job. My mother had a job.
And to feed nine people. She cooked on a wood-burning stove. I don't know how she did it. She
ironed too with a solid piece of iron that was heated on hot coals.*

*I had a good childhood. I went to public school to seventh grade. I went to public school in
the morning from eight am to one pm and cheder* (Jewish religious school) *in the afternoon,
from three pm to six pm. If I had spare time, I would help my father in the shop. I swept the
floor, helped keep things orderly, and did whatever I was told to do. We usually ate dinner at
seven pm.*

*We got around by foot. We walked everywhere. Delivery of our cabinets was done by hired
people who owned a horse and wagon.*

19

Books

Mirla

Although we children never talked about the Holocaust, our parents did when they were with fellow survivors. Unless I asked, they did not speak to me about their experiences. Even then, the answers were short and to the point with no elaboration. However, when the survivors got together, the Holocaust was their primary topic. If I quietly and unobtrusively entered the dining room, where they always sat and talked when they got together, and stood nearby, I could hear their stories, stories they never shared with us or with their American friends. Understanding Polish and Yiddish enabled me to understand them. Each survivor had his and her own unique story, but in each unique story there were the similarities of surviving in one way or another. I do not remember any details of the conversations. I just remember that they would share and compare their experiences before and after the war. I remember when my father reunited with one of the Baum brothers, Salek. Salek, like my father, was from Lodz and deported to Auschwitz when the ghetto was liquidated. They were together in some concentration camps and reminisced. I remember hearing them laugh as they recalled the incident with Willy the Red Nose, a concentration camp guard.

As I got older, my father talked to me more about the war, especially if he had just watched a program about WWII. He loved watching those films. Being imprisoned by the Nazis for nearly six years and in the hermetically sealed Lodz Ghetto for four years, he knew little of what was going on beyond the barbed wires of the ghetto or concentration camps. Films informed him. He was interested in watching Holocaust documentaries and reading about it no matter how gruesome they were. I suppose that, after living the horrors of the Holocaust, watching films and reading about it were not shocking. As the war became more distant in time, books about the Holocaust became more numerous and specific. Survivors wrote their memoirs, researchers published their works, and information from Germany, Switzerland and other European countries that had been kept secret came to light. My dad purchased numerous books about the Holocaust. He loved to sift through them and learn more about that time and what went on behind and beyond the attempted annihilation of the Jews by the Nazis.

On the other hand, I was more interested in my lost family and my parents' experiences during the war. Whenever possible, I would try to audiotape my dad. However, he rarely agreed to allow me to turn on the tape recorder. He would get irritated and say, "Just listen." So instead I would jot down his comments. He was not always agreeable to that either, because it would mean he did not have my undivided attention. But he did not fuss if I continued to write. Years later, when my father was in his late 60s, he volunteered to talk about his Holocaust experiences in the local schools. His talks were factual, providing little in the way of emotional insights. He appreciated talking to students who were respectful, listened to his stories and asked thoughtful questions. He came home irritated if the students misbehaved, did not listen, or asked what he thought were stupid questions, although he did give them leeway since they may not have known better. They were after all, young. It was more unsettling when he complained that the children in Jewish schools were undisciplined and showed little interest in his stories, unlike the audiences in public and Christian schools. At different times, students asked to interview him privately. He was always happy to accommodate them and welcomed them into his home.

My dad would often share the information he learned in the books with me. I listened but found it too emotionally difficult to read those books. One in particular gave chilling accounts of the brutality of the Ukrainians, Lithuanians, and Croatians toward the Jews during the war. After reading *The Good Old Days: The Holocaust as Seen by Its Perpetrators and Bystanders*, by Ernst Klee, Willi Dressen and Volker Riess, he said that I should not read it. It would be too hard for me. There were times that the Germans had to intervene and stop the viciousness that they were witnessing. David Wyman, in his book "The Abandonment of the Jews," gave facts of how an anti-Semitic State Department and certain important statesmen stood in the way of helping European Jewry. I started reading it but stopped after a bit. Learning about the ingrained anti-Semitism at the State Department, which had a direct bearing on their refusal to help European Jewry, was extremely difficult for me. It added to my sorrow and anger knowing that the government of the United States was passively complicit in the murder of most of Europe's Jews and, hence, my family.

One of the books we happened to look at together was Henryk Ross's *Lodz Ghetto Album*. The photographs are disturbing in the two worlds they depict. One world is real and the other is the fantasy of lies that the Nazis had predetermined would be fed to the world while the Jews were being murdered and after the annihilation was completed. Worse, the Jews would be the actors in the fantasy world in which they would shortly be destroyed.

The Lodz Ghetto Album

2/4/05

My dad and I look at the photographs in Ross's Lodz Ghetto Album. I write as he explains what is going on in the pictures.

Dad and I look at a photo of a large wood plank-sided truck.

This is the picture of the trucks that were going to Chelmo. They put gas in them, but it didn't work. I had a friend who packed all of his clothes like he was going away on vacation. The Germans said they were going to be resettled. Actually, they were shipped to Chelmo where they were expected to be dead on arrival, from CO (carbon monoxide) *poisoning. But the Germans found that van poisoning wasn't working too well. The vans would overturn. So they had to think of something else. We lived in a state of denial in the ghetto.*

Among the many horrific pictures of the ghetto are pictures of healthy-looking children, some even chubby, eating, smiling, clean and dressed in nice clothing. Many pictures show adults sitting around nicely set tables, some smoking, all seemingly enjoying life. There are pictures of men dressed in clean suits and women wearing their Sabbath best.

Looking at this picture—these were the select few. Children—my nephew didn't look like this. He didn't show my nephew's picture—he just wanted a piece of bread. Most of the book, it shows from the privileged. Here. Look at that. Where did I see that? I saw skeletons, undernourished, swollen. They were watering down the food to have more. These were the privileged. These they had to put in a book on the Lodz Ghetto? Dignitaries, ghetto dignitaries. Look at this. To me I haven't seen it. I saw hunger and misery and death. He shouldn't have published those pictures. The only thing these privileged people were getting was food. They weren't getting radios, jewelry, they were getting food. They were living a privileged life because they were getting food. The vast majority didn't have it. Clowning around (private pictures chapter). *Who clowned around? They had a good time for a couple hours. I never even knew this existed in the ghetto.*

We look at a picture of the wooden bridge connecting the two main parts of the ghetto. Below the bridge is a Nazi sentry walking with a rifle. On either side of the street below is a wooden fence encased in barbed wire.

You know how many times I went through this bridge? Everyday. I used to walk here in the snow. Freezing. Scared. The guard walked down here. He kept his hands in his pockets— he was freezing too.

22

My dad flips through the pictures and sees more pictures of healthy children.

Look at these children of the privileged. Some denier will look at these pictures and say, 'See it wasn't so bad.' They didn't take a picture of me sitting like this (my father puts his head down, his arms hugging himself) *in the middle of the night waiting for a little bit of soup.*

We see photographs of ghetto Jews, some pulling and others pushing tanks. One woman has a shoe on her right foot and the left is bare, another has rags tied around her feet and a third is barefoot, covered in filth. On the following page is an enormous crater.

See this picture here this was real. They were going around collecting the feces. Before the war on the end of Franciskyanksa there was a big manmade hole in the ground. When the Germans came in the feces were dumped in there. In there they also dumped chlorine for disease. See this picture here this was real. Look at this woman with rags on her feet. They were going around collecting the feces. They didn't live long. The Germans in order for there not to be disease they used to spread chlorine and these people breathed in the chlorine so they didn't live long.

We see more pictures of the privileged, this time a couple of shirtless and athletic looking young men.

Whoever put this book together is an idiot, he had no brains. Look at this. They look like they're going to the Olympics. He didn't have to put this here. The denier will look at this and show this picture and say, "See it wasn't so bad." And this after the survivors will all be dead. The man who put this book together should have his head examined. I was in the ghetto from the first day to the last day. All I saw was misery. Marilyn this looks like they were going to the Olympiad. I saw people their feet swelled up and you press it and the indentation stays there until it works its way up. I went to work in the morning, worked 11 hours, went home, ate a little bit of watered-down soup and worried that the Germans wouldn't kill us. These pictures look like they were in the Riviera. Whoever put this book together shouldn't have put these pictures in. This wasn't the ghetto.

My dad comments on the text accompanying many of the photographs.

In writing he's pretty accurate. But one picture is worth a thousand words—after all it wasn't so bad.

We look at a picture with the remains of one of the two main synagogues in Lodz. One of the Germans' first acts of destruction in Lodz was to demolish the synagogues at the cross section of the main streets, Jidowska and Wolborska. We see the pictures of the synagogue before and after its destruction.

This was the main synagogue. They built the shul, Poznyanski (a Jewish industrialist). He was one of the richest Jews. He built the goyim (Gentiles) a church. He built the Jews a hospital. He donated land and they brought masons from Italy to build the synagogue. When the Germans came in, first they burned it. They put in straw and at night they burned it. When we got up, we saw it burning. But the structure remained standing. The Germans then brought in their own demolishing experts and they dynamited it and these were the pieces that remained of the synagogue—at Jidowska and Wolborska. They burned it in the middle of the night and then later they came and dynamited it and let it lay. This is a chunk left from the synagogue. They were nuts.

The topic of food comes up.

Sometimes they brought in food to Balutski Rinnek and Radogosch. Uncle Leo worked there. The Germans didn't allow the Polaks who brought the food to go into the ghetto. So Jews took over the wagons, unloaded the food, potatoes or whatever. They used to bring in food by railroad cars to Radogosch. They sent in oil; it was stinky oil. It was brown and I don't know what it was made out of. When you used to work in a factory, that's where you used to get a watery soup. Kohlrabi, a worthless vegetable they used to put in the soup. Anything not for human consumption they used to bring to the ghetto. Stinking and rotten potatoes they sent those to the Jews. People who worked in the kitchen they had more soup, no meat, just more soup. You know how many people died from hunger in one winter? Ten thousand people. They couldn't bury them. The ground was frozen. In spring they dug graves. They didn't know who they buried. So many died. The wagon used to go by, pulled by people and pick up dead people. Deceased overnight. Took them away to the cemetery.

As Dad talks about the lack of food, he reminds himself of our trip to Lodz in 1990.

Remember when we went to Lodz, I wanted to go to Chernitzgego. We had a friend, a Polak, Nita. He was a quiet man. He had two children. A girl and a boy. When the Germans came in, they arrested the boy. They killed him and they burned him in Radogodsczcz. The mother found out and she went crazy. Leibish told me after the war. Because Liebish was in Lodz after the war and he told me the mother got insane. They ironed laundry. It was like a big platform and they had heavy rollers and the pressure from the rollers ironed the laundry. He built a one family brick home on Czarnecky. My father helped him buy the lumber. When the ghetto was formed, he had to leave. (Gentiles were told to leave the ghetto. They were told to move into the homes out of which the Jews were forced. The Jews, who were forced out of their homes, had lived in the areas that were not as poor as the area that became the ghetto). *He told my father, "Look you take care of the property"' So when we got it, we made a vegetable garden from the yard. The yard was about a ¼ of an acre. I planted beets, potatoes, those little radishes. And after one season, the second year, Rumkowski came and took it away from us and made a prison—Czarneckego 14 (14 Czarnecky Street). From there they used to transport people out, the undesirables. Once they took the building away from us, we didn't go there no more. I don't know what happened to them.*

The daily life of a Jew in the ghetto was marked by constant hunger, misery and death. However, nothing could compare to the dreaded Gehsperre, also known as aktion. Some photographs show the ghetto Jews soon after a Gehsperre. The Gehsperre was a death sentence for any Jew selected for removal from the ghetto. At the beginning of the war they were gassed at Chelmo. Later, they were murdered on the spot or removed from the ghetto to be killed.

The Gehsperre was when they came and took all the children, twenty thousand, and older people and whoever the Germans felt like taking.

The constant movement in and out of the ghetto meant that Jews taken during the Gehsperre were replaced by Jews deported from other cities and countries. We look at photographs of the deportees with their belongings.

They (Germans) were such thieves. They stole possessions from the Jews. It was unbelievable what they did.

The Germans didn't throw away anything. Did you see in Auschwitz the glasses they kept? (reference to our visit to Auschwitz in 1990)

Chaim Rumkowski was an elderly Jewish man selected by the SS to receive and comply with orders from the Nazis. In a sense, he was the ghetto head. He was a controversial figure. There are several pictures of him. I ask Dad his opinion of the man.

It wasn't Rumkowski's doing to keep the ghetto going, it was the SS. They had labor and for the labor they fed us stinking potatoes. The SS were making money off of us. Rumkowski didn't have a darn thing to say. They came and gave Rumkowski orders. If Rumkowski didn't give enough the Germans went in and took the numbers, they wanted. Once the Germans didn't like something someone said and they beat him up. When they decided they had enough of the Jews all they had to do was ship them off to be killed.

My dad had watched a PBS program on Auschwitz. He spoke about the depiction of Rumkowski in the program.

On the show last night, they had a woman who worked for Rumkowski. She said that he sexually abused her—touched her, you know. How is that relevant to what went on in the ghetto? It's nothing compared to what was going on then. The Germans did such terrible things to the Jews and this woman talks about Rumkowski. Rumkowski was a king with a paper crown. He had no power. Whatever he did he did because he was ordered to do so by the Germans. The Germans had room in their extermination camp, so they said we want fifteen thousand children and Rumkowski had to deliver. He sent around men to round up the children. One woman got so irate she was yelling and giving them a hard time. They rounded up much less than the Germans demanded. So, the Germans went in and did the job themselves. They brutally took children, threw them out of windows, smashed their heads into walls. It was horrible. What was Rumkowski? He was nothing. When the Germans entered the ghetto, the elders of the kehilah (community) *ran away. The Germans happened to see Rumkowski. He looked distinguished—a lot of gray hair, a business suit. So they looked at him and said, 'You're in charge.' That's how he became head of the Lodz ghetto. These were his only qualifications. When Auntie Franka, Hanka and Auntie Eva were in Milhausen* (a notorious concentration camp), *they picked a woman to be in charge of the barrack because she looked good to the Germans—heavy set with big breasts. Those were her qualifications.*

It does not tell the story right this book.

It took me about four years to convince my dad to allow me to videotape him talking about what he went through during the Holocaust. It took as long to convince—I think nag is a better word here—my mother, aunt, uncle and father-in-law to allow me to tape them. Perhaps, they did not want their suppressed emotions to resurface, emotions that were so brutally strong and imbedded in their souls. Perhaps reburying them would be a trying chore. I can understand because talking, reading, or watching programs about the Holocaust makes me feel very emotional. I will not watch a Holocaust movie or program or read a book on the topic after two in the afternoon. It takes that long for my strong emotional reaction to ebb enough so that I can sleep at night.

The Tsunami Arrives

Mirla

In September 1939 the German army marched in the city of Lodz. In February 1940 the Lodz ghetto was formed. The lives of the Lodz Jews would never be the same. Most would be murdered. Every Jewish family, whose roots in Poland had reached deeply and anchored them to this country for hundreds of years, would be forcefully removed and their connection to their land yanked out. An entire culture, ethos, language, Jewish vibrancy and religion were viciously ripped from the entirety of Poland in five short years. To the Jews who lived through this time, five years was a lifetime. Through the ages of history these five years will be but a split second. It took a historical split second to nearly annihilate a people whose claim to live in peace in the region was undeniable yet denied to them.

Poland was a virulently anti-semitic country in the years preceding WWII. Anti-semitism ran through the fabric of Polish society. Polish priests taught their flocks that the Jews had killed Jesus. Being devout Catholics, the Poles accepted this lie as fact. Catholics believed that Jesus suffered for Christians. In turn, the Catholic Poles made sure that the Polish Jews suffered because of Jesus.

Before the war, my dad lived in an area of Lodz that was predominantly Jewish. Among friends and family, Yiddish was the language spoken. They learned Polish in school but spoke that language only when dealing with Christian Poles.

I was curious as to whether my father or his family had suffered at the hands of the Catholics before WWII. My father said that he and his family had few dealings with the Catholic Poles. The Jews tried to avoid them as much as possible. However, interaction was inevitable.

Keren

The rule about living as a Jew in Poland was that you never ventured far away from your Jewish neighborhood. Rarely did any young Jewish child walk alone to school. Rarely did he play alone outside, always in groups of two or more children. For my grandfather, it all began with a cigarette. The ash, smoldered into his skin, searing anti-Semitism into his mind.

He was pressing his nose against the bakery window trying to match the smells wafting outside with the delicious looking desserts inside. An ordinary Polish man stood nearby with his young son and my grandfather thought nothing of it. Focused on the bakery smells, he was not paying attention as the man's footsteps approached him. He did not react when the smell of cigarette smoke began to mask the fresh-baked scents. Then he felt the burn, the singeing, searing pain of a lighted cigarette being dug into his neck. The man smiled as he twisted and turned the cigarette into his skin. My grandfather ran home in intense pain. His four older brothers stormed out of the house, ready to fight a Pole for the first time in their lives. Too late. The man had disappeared in the Polish crowd. But in his absence, he had left a smoldering hole and a memory of what it was like to be Jewish in Poland.

I was in a bakery near my house and there was a Polish guy with a little boy standing there. And he was smoking a cigarette and he burned a hole in my neck.

On August 24, 1939, the war with Germany was imminent. The mayor of Lodz appealed for help digging anti-aircraft ditches. Every citizen rushed out to help. Fifty thousand people dug in a single day. Germany invaded Poland September 1, 1939. That night Poland's air force was decimated. Next, the Polish railroads and communication networks. They bombed Warsaw and Lodz. Air raids were constant. Leon, at 22, was serving in the army, causing additional anxiety for the family. By September 6, the residents of Lodz knew the arrival of the Nazis was imminent.

Itzhak and 15-year-old Gedalia went out for a walk. Gray skies loomed overhead as they forlornly stood and watched endless rows of goose-stepping Nazis parade through Lodz. The sound of their boots smacked the sidewalks as the horses were maneuvered on the streets of stone. Crisp black uniforms darkened the street; a fire red armband with the threatening black swastika wrapped around the bicep of each Nazi swung forward and back like a pendulum gone awry. It took the German soldiers the entire day to walk through Lodz with the their Büssing-NAG trucks, their cannons and the rest of their murderous machinery.

My grandfather and his father watched the Nazi onslaught with trepidation.

The Germans came in and occupied Poland. We couldn't do this and we couldn't do that. You know, life was so hard. Especially for my mother and father.

28

Forbidden

Keren

The principal announced, "There is no more school for Jews." Dead silence filled the room. My grandfather went home. When he opened the door to his apartment earlier than he should have, no one reacted. The end of my grandfather's schooling was the least of everyone's problems. Itzhak no longer had a business, by order of the Germans.

Jews were strictly forbidden from withdrawing more than a set amount from their own bank account.

"By order of the Reich, Jews cannot withdraw more than 250 zlotys from the bank."

Jewish organizations had to relinquish control of all properties and monies to the Nazis.

"By order of the Reich, the property and funds of such Jewish organizations will be under the protection of the German Administration. The same applies to Jewish welfare establishments."

Jews had to abide by strict curfews.

"By order of the Reich all Jews within the Government-General are forbidden to enter or use pathways, streets and public squares between the hours of 9 pm and 5 am without written authority specifying the times and places, issued by the local German authorities. Orders by local German authorities containing more severe restrictions are not affected by this regulation."

Jews were strictly forbidden to operate any business, work in any trade or sell any merchandise.

"By order of the Reich, Jews are forbidden to operate retail stores, mail-order houses, or sales agencies, or to carry on a trade [craft] independently. They are further forbidden, from the same day on to offer for sale goods or services, to advertise these, or to accept orders at markets of all sorts, fairs or exhibitions. Jewish trade enterprises which violate this decree will be closed by the police."

No Jew had the right to refuse forced labor. Germans had the right to confiscate Jewish factories and enterprises and claim them as their own. No Jew had the right to access channels of communication. No Jew had the right to use wagons or pushcarts. He is a brute animal that must carry everything on his body. The Jew must wear the Star of David on his front and back. All these orders were to be followed. Any Jew failing to follow any order was to be executed.

"Every Jew is our enemy in this historic struggle, regardless of whether he vegetates in a Polish ghetto or carries on his parasitic existence in Berlin or Hamburg or blows the trumpets of war in New York or Washington. All Jews by virtue of their birth and their race are part of an international conspiracy against National Socialist Germany. They want its defeat and annihilation and do all in their power to bring it about."

"The Jews are responsible for the war. The treatment they receive from us is hardly unjust. They have deserved it all."

As soon as the Nazis entered Lodz, the Jews were beaten and robbed for doing no more than walking down the street. Jews had to strip for the Nazis. The Jews were German prey, to be played with and tortured, as a cat would do to a mouse.

Life in The Lodz Ghetto

Mirla

After the invasion of Poland, the Germans made one proclamation after another with each further limiting the ability of the Jews to move around, work, own anything, congregate and observe holidays.

In 1990, I videotaped my dad's story of his experiences during the Holocaust.

The directive was that if you did anything, they didn't want you to do, it was punishable by death. Not by prison, death.

Daily life, laws, mores and ethics were turned upside down. Laws and personal rights ceased to exist. Killing of innocents became legal, as long as it was a Jew being killed. Stealing became legal, if one stole from the Jews. Torture of innocents became legal, if the person being tortured was a Jew. The stealing of Jewish property became legal. Overt hatred of Jews was sanctified. There was nothing a German could do that could break a law, moral or legal. The Germans were hallowed by their own decree.

Upon their arrival in Lodz, the Germans began confiscating Jewish property.

We had a friend, he was an acquaintance of my brother. He was taken to the Krippo, the German police. He was in the leather business. He was badly beaten up. Terribly beaten up. He died a short time after.

They hanged a guy here for stealing shoelaces. He made the shoelaces out of his own belt. The Germans killed him for stealing his own belt. The Germans said everything is their property. So he was killed for stealing his own belt. The wife and the children were forced to watch his execution. He was hanged. For making shoelaces from his own leather belt. For a pair of shoelaces, stealing.

Keren

Growing up as the third generation, I could always feel the Holocaust's imprint on me. I was aware that the Holocaust had played an important role in my family history, and I knew I had to remember that fact. Ironically, I never had any emotions towards the Holocaust, never crying or feeling ill when watching or listening to stories of the atrocities. My fifth grade Hebrew schoolteacher tried to get the class to simulate life in Nazi Germany. I asked her, "What's the point? We know the story."

Keren this has to be good. I'm telling you the way it was. Nothing add. A lot of teenagers don't want to do it. They don't want to know. They say, enough already of the Holocaust! But it's important, Keren, right? For posterity.

Keren, you think in different terms. You know, I go to schools and I speak with these kids. And they ask me about Auschwitz, how many times a week did they change the towels? You know? Towels, what are you kidding? There was no such a thing. We didn't see a towel for all the time I was in the camps.

Keren, there was no account, nothing. There was no...you think in different terms. If prisoners died, they took them away. You had to work. You didn't ask questions. It's hard to understand, a regular person, to understand those circumstances.

I'm the third generation; I can't figure out how to tell the story. The trouble is, I'll be the first generation to tell it without a survivor by my side.

On December 10, 1939, the top-secret Nazi strategizing on what to do with Lodz's Jews began. The temporary solution: ghettoize the Jews in the most rundown area of the city. (The Lodz ghetto would become the largest, most isolated one in Europe.)

"The creation of the ghetto is, of course, only a temporary measure. I reserve to myself the decision concerning the times and the means by which the ghetto and with it the city of Lodz will be cleansed of Jews. The final aim must in any case bring about the total cauterization of this plague spot."

Gedalia's family didn't have to march into the ghetto with their belongings dragging behind them in carts and wheelbarrows. His home was already located in the ghetto, close to the wall under construction on Franciskynska Street. Instead, the family watched as day after day streams of Jewish families from other parts of the city and the surrounding areas poured into the ghetto. They heard the cries as the rich families discovered their new dilapidated dwellings. They noticed the tears as dislodged families tried to find a place for their elderly parents, children and belongings. They watched the Germans patrol the never-ending stream of people and belongings. They saw the Catholic Poles drive under the bridge that now connected the two parts of the ghetto

With the establishment of the ghetto the exchange began. Jewish labor for the German people. Jewish labor for food. Jewish labor for less food. Jewish labor for freedom. Jewish labor for a dream. Jewish labor for a myth.

Mirla

In February 1940 the Lodz ghetto was established in the area known as Bałutcki. In the spring of 1940, with snow still on the ground, the ghetto was closed off, hermetically sealed and guarded from the outside world.

We were in a prison. One big cell. Like one big cell. ...I saw once they drove by our house and shots rang out and in front of our house, they killed a Jewish person for no reason. ...You were a sitting duck for them.

Jews were not allowed to have newspapers from outside the ghetto. Radios were forbidden. Disobedience was punishable by death. Jews were forbidden to work outside of the ghetto. Children were forbidden to attend school outside of the ghetto. There was no mail, but ironically, there was a post office. There was no food. Leaving the ghetto to get food was impossible. Hunger became every Jew's constant companion. Jews could eat when the Germans decided they could. If the Germans did not want food to enter the ghetto, it did not. The Germans decided what the Jews could eat and they decided that the Jews would be fed only substandard food; the oil was rancid, the potatoes rotten, the vegetables moldy. The Germans decided how much food the Jews could consume. The determined amount was below subsistence because the Germans had no long-term need for the Jews since the Germans had determined that they were to be annihilated— they were to be wiped off the face of the earth.

There was always hunger from the start of the ghetto. Feet started to swell for some people. Some people got very skinny. There was no medicine. Why would they give medicine? ...They didn't care if you were alive... If you die, no big loss...There were never good times. There were always bad times. Then there were worse times. ...I think the bed bugs left too the ghetto. They didn't have enough to eat. What are they gonna bite?

We ate about two slices of bread a day. Vegetables in summer. You had to manage it; you couldn't eat it at one time. You had to be disciplined. You had to ration yourself because if you ate the food all at one time you didn't have any left for the rest of the week.

You had a watery soup once a day in the factories. Whatever you got you didn't have enough. We used to cut the bread so it was thin like paper. You didn't just swallow it; you used to eat it because you had to chew. If you just swallowed it you missed the chewing. You develop a different behavior pattern.

The biggest problem was lack of food, the hunger. The cramps in your stomach, they demand food. You never had enough food to eat. You ate practically anything you could lay a hand on. The stomach demanded it. But was nothing there. No chicken. No eggs. We forgot what a chicken looked like. There were no dogs, cats, no rats in the ghetto. No birds. There was nothing to eat.

The Germans made sure that before entering the ghetto the Jews would have nothing that would be of any value. Those goods, in their perverted upside down newly established standards, the Germans claimed as their own. If it was illegal for a Jew to own any item of value, then in the German upside-down immoral world, it was not stealing to steal from the Jews.

To improve my concept of daily life in the Lodz ghetto, I asked my dad if they had rudimentary items, like soap.

There were no soap. Maybe once in a while you used to get a piece of soap. There was no hot water. There was no soap to wash your clothes. There was practically nothing...Toilet paper? Aw come on! There was no place to buy a shirt, to buy shoes. If someone passed away and left shoes, you could buy the shoes. In the ghetto there were no animals. There were no rats. There were no cats. There were no birds. There were no dogs. You didn't see a chicken. You didn't see a dog. You didn't see a cow, a horse. It was like the penitentiary. They locked the door and you didn't see anything.

It's hard for you to understand. There was no papers. There was no radio. There was no form of communication. You had your troubles. The hunger was constant.

As I write this, my breathing starts to get shallow. I feel my stomach start to knot as my emotions rise.

In 1940-41 the Germans started to demand people. They never said for what. They took the people that didn't have jobs. Families that didn't have work. Some people volunteered at the beginning. People had it so bad. How bad can it be? You're starving here, in this place the ghetto, Lodz, so you'll starve there. ...They were lied to by the Germans. They were told they were being resettled. They were never told the truth. They didn't know what it was waiting for them there. We weren't told they had extermination camps and they were doing all these bad things. They probably died.

The German war machine tore through Europe decimating the Jewish population everywhere the Nazi annihilators set foot. But what to do with all those Jews? On the spot murder was not always feasible. One solution was ship these Jews to the Lodz ghetto as Lodz ghetto Jews were being shipped out of the ghetto for extermination. The new ghetto prisoners were not prepared for the sudden traumatizing shift that awaited them in the ghetto.

When they used to ship out people they brought in people from outlying areas. And they brought in people from Prague, Czechoslavakia, Germany, from Austria. They brought them in from little shtetlachs, little towns. The Jewish administration would tell them where to go. When they came in it hit them. A lots of them died. They couldn't adjust themselves in such a short time to the conditions. Where they came from there was food. And here when they came they were given a little soup, watered soup and a piece of bread and from this they had to live. Or they gave them for two weeks food that a person could eat it in one meal. They had to manage for two weeks. And they were disoriented, dislocated and the winter was cold; there was no fuel and a lot of them couldn't make it.

The Lodz ghetto was a manufacturing community. There were metal works, clothing manufacturing, woodworking and other factories where the Lodz Jews were enslaved and worked to provide supplies for the German war machine and economy. My father, his brothers and his father worked in the woodworking factory called the Holzgalanterie.

I worked at the Lodz Ghetto, at the Holzgalanterie, from the day the ghetto was formed up until the final liquidation in August 1944. I worked as a Tischler operating a band saw. I cut out wooden platforms for shoes, crib parts and wooden toys. I worked ten hours a day, six days a week. Other than one day per week, we were given no other days off during the entire fours years in the ghetto. I worked night shifts and day shifts. We were allowed one 30-minute break during the entire ten-hour shift. We were paid substitute German money that could be used only in the ghetto.

My father had compared the enclosure of the Jews in the ghetto to imprisonment. To the extent that they were sealed off from the outside world, that comparison is apt. However, in the United States prison system, inmates are fed three meals a day, whether they work or not, and earn some money for their work. In the ghetto, the Jews had to work in order to eat. Work got the Jews a meager ration of a small loaf of bread that had to last two weeks and daily watery soup in the factory. Sugar was on occasion brought into the ghetto. In the summer, vegetables, often rotten, were allotted. That was it. If that was not enough to keep one alive, that's how it was.

We were slaves without food. We were worse than slaves. A slave is good taken care of. You see if you had a slave you paid for the slave. It's something that you own so you had to take care. We were worse than slaves. We were worthless. They got us for nothing. And if you get it for nothing it's worth nothing to them. In the United States the slaveholder used to take good care on the slave because he was an asset. Maybe he used to slap him or he used to do something but basically he used gave him food because he didn't feed this slave he couldn't perform the work right. In those days we were worse than slaves because we had to work and we didn't get anything. The life expectancy was so long [translation: the life expectancy became extremely short due to the deprivations] *and then they got somebody else…They didn't care how long you gonna live. And the shorter the better. And if you didn't die they killed you anyway. They used you as much as they can. They kept you because they couldn't kill everybody in the same time. So they made the best use out of you. And when the time came they would kill you anyway.*

Gradually, news of the demise of European Jews began to trickle into the ghetto. Needless to say, the news was disturbing in the extreme. The ghetto inhabitants knew that the situation for Jews was bad, but they didn't want to believe it was as horrendous as what they heard. The Jews in the ghetto relied on denial to keep them living day to day so as not to extinguish hope in their prospects for survival.

We all knew what situation we are. But we had to make the best out of it otherwise we would have gone nuts. Would have gone crazy. Certain things that you heard you didn't want to hear. Such as they would say they were sending Jews out to the frying pan. But you didn't want to know what it is. We heard little things, bits and pieces. Not in the beginning. By the end of the ghetto we heard atrocities were being committed and they have camps, but it wasn't substantiated. It was one man telling the other man. There was some connection with the outside world, I don't know how. And if you heard something bad you didn't want to believe it because otherwise was like in the end what you gonna do? If you wanna believe it that they're gassing people or they're burning people, if that's the case then tomorrow it might be you. So you didn't want to believe it. You exclude it from your mind. It's not so. We always thought maybe maybe maybe somehow the war will come to end and we'll survive. We lived from day to day.

The Germans did not come into the ghetto unless it was for a specific purpose. One such purpose was the feared and dreaded geshperre or aktion. The geshperre occurred episodically in the ghetto. When a geshperre was announced, Jews were forced to remain in their homes until the Germans had finished their business in the ghetto. Their business, during a Gehsperre, was to go from house to house and forcefully remove the inhabitants they felt no longer should remain in the ghetto. The aktion could last days on end. During aktions, the Germans came in and took the groups of people who they felt were worthless because they could not produce. Among the first groups targeted were older people and children.

Fear was only when they made the gehspeere, the aktion. All sperres were bad. And while the Sperre was going on you have a lump in your stomach that didn't want to go away til it passed. Sometimes it took 10 days. There was no work while the Sperre was going on. Before [the Gehsperre was to start] *they gave us for eight days food. And this food had to last for the Gehsperre. People who didn't have self-control didn't survive.*

Everybody was under curfew with nobody going to work. The Germans came into the ghetto during aktions and went house to house. They could take 20,000 people in an aktion. When the Germans got their allotted number of people the aktion stopped.

They went from block to block to block. Systematically. Once they picked out my father. They took him to a central place where they used to ship them out. We managed to get him out of there. In the factory where he worked, he was a good craftsman so we get him out. The next Sperre, which was the next action a year later, they took my married sister. We took her out too. We got her out. My mother was, they had a Sperre and the SS man came in, a young fat guy. He came with a machine gun. He started to select. He selected my mother to go to the right. While he was selecting other people moving ahead, we told my mother to go the left and we put her behind us. Mother remained with us. They didn't brutalize. They wanted to keep it as quiet as possible and as orderly. If they would start shooting and brutalizing, people would hide and they would be more afraid to stay and be selected, they would avoid it and they would have to look for these Jewish people.

Did people try to hide?

We did hide a lots of instances. But lots of times you couldn't hide. You can't hide 100 people. There was not only us. There was a lots of people in the apartment house. Where you gonna hide? You can hide two, three, 10 people but where can 100 people hide? Sometime an individual, but not as a group.

What about children?

There were no children allowed in the ghetto so they were not treated as children. There was once an order that they took out all the children. They made a Sperre, they took out all the children and all the older people, so actually no children should have been in the ghetto after that but there were still children in the ghetto. If a mother didn't want to give up her child they killed the mother.

Yossel, my dad's nephew, was born just before the establishment of the ghetto. While in the ghetto, his parents had to work in order to get food. So, from the age of two, Yossel was left alone in the apartment. He was one of the children not found during the aktion. I asked Dad what these children did and if they wandered while the adults were working.

For some reason those children didn't wander. They understood what was going on. There was no place to go. He didn't leave the apartment. He stayed by himself. It's hard for you to understand. You know, children you get together. There was none of those things. Everyone was for himself. It was in the morning, she [Yossel's mother] had to go to work. And then probably lunchtime she came home and then went back to work. We couldn't help. Everybody had to work. There was no such a thing like sharing. There was nothing to share.

The Nazis took great pleasure out of tormenting the enslaved ghetto Jews and were cruelly inventive in various ways.

There were always bad things going on, never good. Not enough that they killed people. They tormented them. Open hunting season all the time. The Germans built gallows. They made the Jews near the gallows watch the hangings. Those hanged were left there for a few days. On Yom Kippur they always had some surprise. They used to hang people on Yom Kippur you know on Passover. That was the present for the Jewish people.

The evil of the German war machine had no boundaries. As long as the Germans were the sole perpetrators, lies, deceit, murder, torture, and theft became the acceptable immoralities that invaded Europe. The Nazis ripped and shredded humanity and kindness out of the fabric of life wherever they set foot. They forced good people into enemy status. They allowed hateful people to thrive, as long as the haters tormented and killed Jews. For the Jews, this meant that there was not a place where they could feel safe and protected from the Nazi scourge. There is no easy reference point to understand what the European Jews faced. Perhaps those unfortunate enough to be passengers on a hijacked plane may understand. If they attack the hijackers, they will die. If they don't attack, they may die. But they have nothing to attack with while the hijackers have machine guns and grenades. Sitting duck passengers. People whose only crime was to be on the plane. Jews whose only crime was to be Jewish in Europe.

Among the thousands of Jews who died in the ghetto were my grandfather and an uncle.

Hirsch died in the beginning of the ghetto. I don't know what he died of. We got a doctor. Hirsch died a couple of hours later. The doctor said he was very bad. Then we had another death. My father died in 1943. He died from hunger. They're buried in the cemetery in Lodz. Lodzer Jewish Cemetery.

So many people died there was no time to mark them. And if they marked, the mark disappeared. There was no, there was a breakdown in administration, so many people dying and so many problems and I don't think they bothered to mark the graves. We all attended the burial. There were separate graves. They buried them one by one. It was a full time job to take care of all the dead.

The Liquidation

Mirla

In August of 1944, the final of the final solutions for the Jews of the Lodz ghetto was instituted. Piece by piece the ghetto was liquidated. After four and a half years in the ghetto, the Jews, who had struggled daily to survive, were sent to Auschwitz for extermination.

Before the liquidation of the ghetto, a German officer came to the ghetto to tell the Jews that because the war was coming near that they were going to be resettled to another place, for their safety. That another place needed their work. The German made sure to mention that what he was telling the Jews was no lie. And we should take the pots and pans with us because of the war they will not be able to give us pots and pans. And we should take anything that's of any of value we should take with us. To fool us they lied to us. He told the Jews where to report to. People didn't believe them and that's why they didn't wanna go. They took us forcefully. They used to come to the house, the SS man and they used to force us to go and they forcefully put us on the train.

Dad's family did not go for selection. They hid, with another family, in a second-floor apartment that had three rooms in railcar style, one behind the other. Dad made a bookcase that they put in front of the third room so one could not tell that the third room was there. To avoid being selected, he and his family used to crawl through the space into the third room. Once the Germans had looked in each apartment of the building, they left. The Germans stopped the raids at five in the evening. Once five came the family returned to their apartment.

They hid behind the bookcase every day for the entire day. One day, when it was eerily quiet outside, the man of the other family decided go outside. He was spotted by an SS man who wanted to take him away. He told the SS man that he wanted to go with his family. My father and his family saw the man and SS coming. They could have left the hiding place so as not to be discovered. But dad said they were very scared and did not know what to do.

We didn't prepare ourselves for eventualities. What we'll do in case like this or case like this. We didn't have tunnels. We didn't have sewers to escape. We didn't have where to escape. If we had escaped to the Polish side the Polaks would have killed us.

On August 27, 1944, my grandmother Mirla, two aunts, Haya and Leah, young cousin Yossel, uncles Leon and Shmiel and my father were put on a train and shipped out to Auschwitz.

We were brought to Maryshin, put in cattle cars in the train. It was an overnight journey. The next morning, early, it was getting like daylight when we got to Auschwitz.

I ask about food.

No food. What's the matter with you?

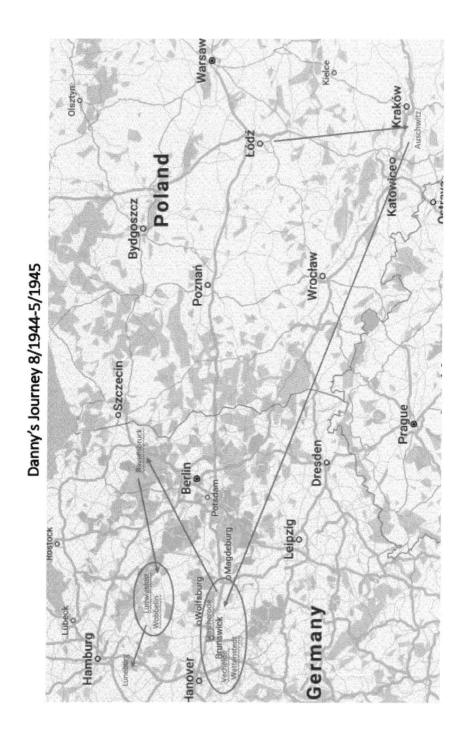

Danny's Journey 8/1944-5/1945

42

Hell On Earth

When they got to Auschwitz/Birkenau the Germans threw open the cattle car doors.

That's when the terror began. We didn't know where we were taken to. There were the SS people with dogs. There were the prisoners. There were Jewish prisoners that could talk Yiddish. They made us get out of there real fast. Everything was fast. You didn't wait. Everything was done real fast. The selection started right there.

An SS man made men go to the right, women to the left and children and older people to a different place. As soon as the selection was completed the prisoners were marched away from the area. This was the last time my dad saw his mother, sisters and nephew.

I think about my father being forcefully herded away from the women in his family and his young nephew. No goodbyes, no hugs. Just German Shepherds growling and baring their fangs. Rifles. Shouts of SCHNELL SCHNELL-FAST FAST as the cattle cars are emptied of Jews. Shots are fired. He will never see them again. Instead, he will see the smoke of their burned bodies waft up from the crematoria. I never asked my father how he dealt with that memory. I imagine myself asking him that question and start to cry. I cry because I know that my father would have gotten too upset with me. Maybe he would have cried at the memory. My father-in-law cried when he remembered the last time he saw his mother as they were transported out of the ghetto. I do not think I could have handled upsetting my father by asking him to express his emotions about such a horrendous moment.

And there was real terror. When we got to the camp and they took over, the inmates looked to see whether we got hidden on the body some other diamonds. They threatened if they're gonna find we have something hidden we're gonna be hanged. He was a Jewish kapo. He just walked around, this kapo, was just beating up people. This wasn't so important if you got hit. It was just the terror. You found out that you're in Auschwitz.

In Birkenau, my father became prisoner 50864. To the Nazis, he was no longer Gedalia Geclewicz, because names were for humans and Jews were subhuman.

After they were disinfected and shaved, from head to toe, they were given striped shirts and pants. The clothes were handed to them without regard to how they fit. The prisoners were left to exchange clothing with each other when what they were given did not fit.

When we got to Birkenau, they took away all our clothes. They stripped everybody. We were shaven, everything. All the body hair, everywhere. Then they disinfect us. You were issued uniform or other clothes. The prisoner's garb, we got a striped uniform. They gave you a shirt, a pair of pants. No underwear. It didn't even matter what fit or didn't fit. So, you had to exchange it with another.

They asked an old prisoner how one got out of Auschwitz. He pointed and said through the chimney. They could see the crematorium. It was a red brick building with black smoke belching out of the chimney.

The kapos gave a threatening speech to the new inmates. This was accompanied by beatings if the prisoners didn't stand correctly, for anything, for nothing.

There were appels, roll call, where everyone had to line up. You had to stay for an hour. And if anything didn't add up, they counted us you know, til everything didn't add up we would stay and they used to make certain exercises, punishment exercises. If someone didn't stay proper in the line everybody had to do exercises. You had bend down, knee bends and stretch your arms out and sit there like for 10 minutes. If you fell, they beat you. There was such a terror there. And until they had everything, everything was tallied, all the prisoners, the amount of prisoners and nobody escaped.

The prisoners were told which block would be theirs. All the prisoners slept on the bare concrete floor. The building was an empty rectangular building. The toilet, rows of concrete with holes, that everyone used, was in another barrack.

You could hardly stretch out. If you slept, you had to sleep on somebody else's body. In other words, if you slept your body was laying on somebody's chest or his leg was laying on your body.

Each daybreak, the prisoners were chased out of the barracks through a single door.

They chased us out fast. And some were standing by the door and you had to move fast. If we didn't go fast some they used to hit like cattle. Have you seen how they move cattle here through a one door opening, a bunch of cattle they have prods? There they had sticks. They used to hit the people to move faster. There was always constant beating going on.

44

In the morning they gave us coffee, if you could call it coffee. Brown water. For the day we got one piece of bread and a soup. That was all. A soup and a piece of bread and in the morning, it was coffee no sugar and this was it.

I asked Dad if he had to work in Auschwitz.

They took us once in a while, took us just meaningless work. They took us just to walk a couple of miles, and they put a bunch of grass, you know sod, to move and to carry it from one place to another. Meaningless duties. A couple of times they took us in the morning, they maked [us do] the squats; they walked us some distance and then we walked back. Meaningless.

Meyer had not been hiding with them. He had been transported out a day or two earlier than the rest of the family. On the third or fourth day after they had arrived at Auschwitz, the brothers found Meyer.

To get out of Auschwitz, my father, Meyer, Leon and Shmiel broke the family pact that they had made in the ghetto—never volunteer for anything. Their reason for doing whatever they could to leave was simple: Nothing could be worse than Auschwitz where the sky was black from human ash. This inferno made them desperate to get out at all costs. Büssing NAG was looking for metal workers to work in their factory, so they sent over a German civilian representative to select workers. (Bussing was constructing camps in the Braunschweig area to fulfill the need for skilled metal workers to handle the increased demand in production of vehicles for military use. Foreign civilian workers into the German economy had slowed to a trickle. So, faced with the prospect of a severe labor shortage, two Büssing representatives traveled to Auschwitz to select 1,000–1,200 prisoners fit for work.) The only qualification was how the prisoner looked. If he looked good enough, was young, and the representative felt the company could, as Dad put it, "Get some work out of you," he was selected. Although they had no metal work experience the brothers volunteered. The first batch of some 350 prisoners, who had passed selection, departed for Braunschweig in the middle of September 1944. This group consisted almost exclusively of Polish Jews from the Lodz ghetto. About 100 men from this transport were provisionally assigned to the Mascherode camp. Again, they were stripped of all their clothes, told to shower, and were given striped uniforms: underpants, a striped jacket, pants and a pair shoes. They were given a piece of dark bread and put in the boxcar of a train. The bread each prisoner was given before the journey had to last the three days.

For the journey, the Geclewicz brothers and 50 other men were packed into a single cattlecar, about half the size of an American boxcar. The first men in sat against the dark, black wall and spread their legs open, shifting their bottoms to keep the hard floor from crushing their bony frames. The next men in sat between the spread legs of the other men before spreading their legs. And so it went until the cattle car was packed with the maximum number of prisoners who could be crammed in uncomfortably together. They were on the train for three days with a pail for the excrement. Water for the prisoners was brought onboard only when the train stopped.

Dad, Uncle Leo, Meyer, Schmiel, their brother-in-law and friends from Lodz, the Baum brothers, were all together. They arrived at the German town of Braunschweig, the site of the Büssing NAG factory.

We got some satisfaction. We saw Braunschweig was bombed already. We saw the burned out buildings and devastation. Braunschweig was already bombed and we felt good about it because we saw the war's going on and they're getting clobbered.

Two young SS men guarded the prisoners as they waited. They were carrying whips that they used on any prisoner who, as Dad put it, "Stepped out of line." Stepping out of line meant that if the guard felt like whipping someone, he did.

You didn't have to do anything. On a whim he felt like hitting someone, he hit.

Trucks came and took the prisoners to a small camp in Braunschweig called Mascherode. There the prisoners slept on wood plank boards, stacked like bookshelves.

The lager eldester was a German criminal. He knew that we came from Auschwitz and that people were gassed. He used to kid us, 'You want to write letters to your family?'

The factory food given to the prisoners was a big improvement. At this camp, the prisoners got a sandwich with something like liverwurst on it, two big slices of bread and coffee. For lunch the prisoners were given soup. Supper was another piece of bread with something on it.

Keren
At this camp worked Big Bertha. She and Willy the Roden Naser (Willy the Red Nose) became close. She arranged for him to have a key to the warehouse that would allow him to leave and visit her apartment. One very smart Jew took

the key and sculpted a copy by hand using scraps of metal from the factory. Every night he too would escape. But he had no interest in a fat German lover. Each night, he stole to a nearby farmer's field to scrounge for potatoes. One night, and this is where my grandfather begins to laugh, the Jew was returning from the potato field and the German was heading to his rendezvous with Big Bertha. With the utmost care, each silently put his key into the keyhole. They each turned their keys, but nothing moved. The Jew jerked his key out, afraid that he had been discovered, fearfully looked around him for the Nazi with the gun. The German on the other side of the door did not know what to think. He had been sneaking out for weeks with the same key. Could the Nazis have changed the locks? The Jew ducked into the field and ran behind a wall just as Willy managed to unlock the door. He stepped out and rushed hurriedly away. The Jew watched him go and just as quickly he snuck back in, breathing huge sighs of relief. This two-way traffic continued for a while until the farmer realized his potatoes were disappearing. He waited up one night and chased the Jew back to the camp. Unable to catch him, he went to the camp commander.

All the Jewish prisoners were chased out of the barracks. They were ordered to strip and stand at attention. Their breaths clouded the winter air. They stood for hours as the farmer walked up and down the long rows, looking for the guilty Jew. The man he fingered was ordered by the German commander to receive 100 lashes. Willy suddenly jumped forward, telling the commander that he would gladly take care of the Jew and administer the 100 lashes. My grandfather begins to laugh again. Willy tells the Jew, "Listen, I'm not going to hit you with this whip. I'm going to hit the table. But you better scream as loud as you can in pain." The Jew screamed without receiving a lash on his back.

Roll call…one never knew what exactly to expect when the Nazis forced everyone awake at midnight. Frequently, the purpose was purely to torture the Jews. One night my grandfather was chased out of the barrack and out into the cold snow. The wind whipped around him and the other prisoners. BEND YOUR KNEES, STAND IN A SQUAT UNTIL WE TELL YOU TO STOP. WE SHOOT WHOEVER CANNOT STAND AS WE COMMAND! So, my grandfather, in his thin prisoner stripes and wooden clogs, lowered his bottom closer to the snow. As the merciless winter winds lashed his body, my grandfather raised his hands straight out before him as demanded. Wisps of emaciated human beings haunted the night in a squat position for an hour, two hours, maybe. Thousands of shaven, emaciated men who were minutes before standing straight as a rod in an endless crowd of lines bent their knees so their thighs were parallel to the ground as the obsessive Germans commanded. They slowly stretched their arms out and squatted in that position for who knows how long.

Mirla

My father and his brothers were at Mascherode for a short while. On September 11, they were trucked 15 km outside of Braunschweig to Vechelde. There the prisoners lived in one big room. The prisoners slept on mattress-less wooden bunks. The prisoners had blankets and slept two to a bunk, just enough room to lie down but little room to turn. Across the yard from the prisoners' room was the factory. The block eldester was another German criminal and he had a helper.

The block eldester, he was a mean character. When you used to go for lunch, to get soup, if you didn't hold the bowl the way he liked it, he hit you with the metal ladle in your face so he bloodied you, knocked you out your teeth. So when they used to come back to work, and there were always a lots of bloody faces and you had to work. The German administration complained that the people cannot work because they're getting beaten and they exchanged him. They took this guy away. They sent us another guy which this guy was already better. He didn't abuse people.

At the Büssing factory in Braunschweig, the prisoners were fed by the factory, not the SS. As a result, they got the same sandwiches that the French or Italian forced workers were getting. At the Vechelde location, the factory paid the SS for the work of the Jews. As a result, the allotment and quality of food deteriorated. They now got one piece of thin black bread a day. The soup again became very thin. Their diet reverted to the one they had at Birkenau.

People were so eager for the soup. The soup was like water. The bottom was thicker, so when you mix, the heavy stuff goes to the bottom. If you're the first you get the water. This played a big part. You see, you cannot, you think in different ways. You manipulate how to get a little more food. The thicker the soup the more nourishing it was.

Starvation increased and more people died from hunger. My Uncle Schmiel became sick and stopped working. When Dad returned to the prisoners' room one day, Schmiel was gone. My Uncle Schmiel died from hunger in the winter of 1945.

We worked in the factory. We lived about 350 people living in a room across from the factory. We slept like the sardines. If they could save the stink. Nine months 350 people lived together in a small space and didn't shower. The Germans in the camps couldn't stand the stink.

You got a soup a day and piece of bread in the evening. No medicine period. Shmiel died in this camp. He was not the only one. A lots of people died. They used to strip them. There used to come a truck and take them away. Where they took them I don't know.

And it was filth. There was no toilet paper and paper towels. And there was no normal things people need. No showers. Conditions were terrible. We all must have stunk like hell. Lice developed in Vechelde. You know, from the dirt. Everybody got lice. Lice, they bite. Lice are terrible. Lice, they don't let you sleep. They bite the flesh. And they were big. There the dying started. People started dying from the lack of food. I came home from work and I went to look and they told us Shmiel passed away. From hunger…I don't know. And every day a lots of them died. And they were taken away.

Once, Dad was walked to a nearby town to get something. The German residents saw him but were apathetic. They showed no sympathy. They passed dad like he was invisible. Dad guesses that he weighed about 100 pounds. He was 20 years old.

Keren

In Vechelde, a boil the size of a golf ball bubbled up under my grandfather's skin. The pain immobilized his arm. But what could my grandfather do? He had to keep working at that Büssing-NAG metal press. Gazing around, while struggling to ignore the pain that ripped into his nerves every time he lifted his arm to work the press, Gedalia spotted a scrap piece of metal lying on the floor. He placed the metal to his skin close to the boil, pressed down, slicing through the golf ball sized abscess. Puss and fluid poured from the open wound. When the flow stopped, my grandfather squeezed the remainder of the white custard out with his other hand. When he told me this story, he pointed to the faint white scar, the size of a nickel that marks the spot of the boil.

My grandfather also showed me the scars on his fingers. One day, in Vechelde, he was working the metal press mechanically, automatically and numbly. Arms up, arms down, lift, press, hands in, hands out. This time, though, his hand got too close and the skin on his bony fingers melted into liquid. It hurt like hell. The lice moved to the open wound. My grandfather had no bandages, no iodine, no antibiotic cream. He wrapped the wound in discarded newspaper pieces. A few days later, infection set in. A prisoner told my 20-year-old grandfather to pee on his hand. He urinated on the ripped-up flesh left on the bone. The skin around his wound tightened as the wind whipped it cold. He reached for the gooseneck lamp near his workstation and directed the heat from the light bulb onto his severed skin. His hand throbbed as the heat touched the bone and melted the damaged flesh. Eventually the wound healed, leaving the scars as testimony.

I heal good. Mine personally. This what happened to me.

There was never an escape. In Vechelde, two boys escaped. A farmer invited them into his home to eat. He called the police. They were never seen again. The camp commander called everyone out for roll call and the standing began. Escape is futile, the commander declared. But a lesson is going to be taught. He introduced a barber. The men of Vechelde were to be shorn. It had been months since the prisoners had been shorn in Auschwitz. This barber was ordered to shave a strip of hair off the top of each head. My grandfather, Leon and the others Jewish prisoners had a strip of baldness down the middle of their heads, like skunks.

At this camp, Jews began to feel the war against Germany approaching, hitting close to them.

In March, we lived through some bombings. They were bombing, the Allies, bombed Braunschweig, and we felt good about it. Because we could see from far away that Braunschweig was burning. Then we had air raids. There was next to us was the town of Wattenstadt. There they had a big munitions factory, Hermann Goering Werk, and they came one Sunday, a real lots of American planes, and they bombed this factory. They flew right over us but we didn't care, we felt good because we saw the Germans are being punished. We could have all been killed.

During the air raid the Germans made the prisoners go into the shelter. My grandfather didn't know why they did this.

That's how they protected us. That's how it worked. Into the Schutzkeller, the air raid shelter. They forced you to go there. We didn't want to go. We were laying on the bunk and to walk down into the nasty wet, the nasty basement. A lot of time we hid and they were walking around, you know their helpers and looking for anybody not left behind. There was no rhyme or reason for these things.

Mirla
March 24, 1945, the prisoners were marched from Vechelde to Wattenstadt. The prisoners wore nothing more than the clothes they wore everyday: cotton jacket, pants and wooden shoes. In the cold, they were marched the entire day and night. During the march, Meyer became delirious.

They marched us out the next day. Meyer marched too. Meyer was already on the last. Meyer couldn't make it. Then in the middle he couldn't walk anymore. Meyer was skin and bones when we were forced to march to Wattenstadt. Like a walking skeleton. You know, you see a walking skeleton walks around with the skin holds him together like you seen in those pictures. All of a sudden it hit him. Was like it hit a lots of guys. That they were good good til it hit 'em once and that was the end of it. Meyer was at that stage. They put him on a truck. They put him on a truck but he died. Meyer died in Wattenstadt. He's buried in Wattenstadt. He was buried and has a gravestone. The mayor of Wattenstadt gave the people who died there markers. He was afraid that when the Allies came if they would see mass graves so he buried the dead separately. Meyer has his own marked grave.

At first, Dad didn't know what had happened that caused Meyer to become delirious. The other inmates told Dad about the soup.

The day before the German SS man made him drink a soup and he put in a lots of salt to punish him for something. Because he thought he wanted to steal. The German put out a soup to cool and Meyer was walking by and I don't know if he wanted to take some of the soup or not. Whatever. But the German saw him walking by and called him over and he put in a lots of salt in the soup and he made him drink it. And after he drunk, I found out, I didn't know that, Meyer got delirious.

Keren

My grandfather and Leon were the only members left of the Geclewicz family.

The Nazis, in their desperation, had begun to move the Jews to other camps, away from the approaching Allies and Russians. Men were, once again, herded up and jammed into the cattle cars. Filth, feces, urine and lice were their constant companions. Two days later, they arrived at Neuegamer, but were not allowed entry. The camp was full. The precious cargo moved on to Ravensbrück, the infamous women's concentration camp, on April 16.

The food allotment for the three-day trip to Ravenbrück was a one-and-a-half by four-inch piece of bread. When the train made stops, water was brought onto the train. To their credit, the Jewish prisoners did not steal each other's bread or forcefully take bread from another prisoner.

When they got to Ravensbrück they were brought into a room to get their food allotment. On the other side of the room were inmates who had not come on the train. The place was in disarray. Pushed into the food lines, my grandfather and his fellow Lodz prisoners were given a single piece of bread. Cradling the bread, my grandfather wanted to be careful not to lose a single crumb. Gingerly, he took the bread the Nazis gave to him. Walking away from the line, another emaciated prisoner attacked my grandfather for his bread. The two men struggled. The snow crunched beneath their wooden clogs. My grandfather clutched the bread, refusing to let go. The stranger gave up. My grandfather unclutched his hand; his first meal in five days had disappeared onto the floor in a pile of crumbs. There was no possibility of getting another slice. Dulled, starved, weakened and filthy my grandfather turned from the bread line. Before the war, the Nazis had declared that the Jews were filthy. Filth is what the Nazis had managed to turn the Jews into.

In Germany it was the end. There was no more work anymore. They were protecting us. I don't know what they were trying to do with us. For us they had trains, for German soldiers they didn't have any trains. We were a very important commodity. I don't know what kind of commodity. Really. You think I'm kidding you? Why did they schlep us from Wattenstadt to Ravensbrück? What for? That what, we were important for the war machine? Because Braunschweig was liberated earlier and the allies were nearing to Braunschweig, they evacuate us. Their army was retreating they took us with them. What for? I cannot explain it. The whole thing was sheer stupid. This was the most stupidest thing. Not just us. There was lots of movement. They were moving, all the prisoners they were taking with them. Especially the concentration camp inmates. I don't know about the prisoners of war.

At Ravensbrück they got Red Cross food packages. The packages were from the United States: cheese, coffee, chocolate and different kinds of dried food that had to be cooked. The inmates did not have a stove nor pots or pans. They could not eat the food but they had to protect it and take it with them wherever they went.

We got packages from Red Cross that Germans handed out. Those packages didn't do us any good. They gave us coffee. How do you brew coffee? You need a stove to make the coffee. So it was useless the coffee. They gave us cheese, fat cheese. You ate it you got the diarrhea. We need plain simple bread. The whole package, everything was a joke.

We ate but then another thing. We got packages for some reason there wasn't water for three days in the camp. There was no water. Your tongue was like a piece of leather. Now we got those packages and a lotsa people died from those packages. Because they were not used to eat that cheese. To this day I don't eat American cheese. That was not my food. Simply, I didn't take to it. They had chocolate so you ate a little piece of chocolate. But the first day you needed to drink and you didn't have water.

You know what, I was in the camp I never had a cold. You know that it was so cold, terrible cold, you couldn't move your joints were frozen, your knees, you were so stiff. It was so cold that you got stiff. You were stiff, really stiff. Remarkable, through all the camp that I was in, I didn't have a toothache.

Mirla

At one point, my father and Uncle Leon were put into a barrack next to a women's barrack. The Red Cross, they were told, would do some sort of a prisoner exchange and help the Jews get to Sweden. One morning my father woke up and the women prisoners were gone. He dragged himself out of bed and rushed outside for the roll call. He stood for hours that day with no way out.

It was the first time that you could be men and women so close together. We stayed there but something went wrong. And we didn't go to Sweden. The prisoners were put on a train again. We had to schlep the packages too. For two days or three days. Because the train didn't travel like, the Allies used to bomb. So they traveled mostly during the night. We were shot up by the Allies too. There was a father and a son, they were killed. They shot up the train. The American planes saw a train moving and they shot up the train. Our boxcar just happened not to get hit.

That was a bad concentration camp. We got there with the packages, again (Red Cross packages). We saw there Salek. We hadn't seen him since Wattenstadt. Wattenstadt they took 'em away. We were lined up in Wattenstadt, they made an appel. They didn't tell us but a rumor went around that they're gonna send out people for work. So they used to line us up, 50 people in a block, five deep and ten in a row so 50 50 50 (Dad gestures). And I was in the back. And as we're going, I said Leon let's move. As they were getting closer, we moved away. Eventually, we snuck into the barrack away from this. Once they got their people, they marched them away. That was when we were separated from Salek and Yaakov. We didn't see what happened to them. They took them to another work camp. When we got to Vebelin, they were there! They came a couple days before. They were in a terrible camp. A lots of them didn't make it from those people. They were killed by inmates too, you know, while they were going by train. The Germans were paying other inmates to kill them. They gave them a piece of bread to kill. That's why when we were traveling, we always kept together, only Jews. So always when it came to appel, to line up we always lined up together, 50 together, our own people.

Jewish prisoners were afraid of the Christian prisoners. Once the Jews were among the Christians, the Christians would take away the bread of the Jews. This was especially true if the Jew was outnumbered by Christians. For instance, if they were outnumbered in a box car, the Christians would, as Dad put it, "Finish you." In the reverse situation, if the Jews outnumbered the Christians, they did not take advantage or kill or harm anyone.

53

A matter of fact, we were marching in Ravenbrück and a guy is marching with me. He was a stranger and I got talking to him and he spoke Yiddish. He said, 'I'm not a Jew. I'm a Polak.' He grew up in Warsaw in a Jewish neighborhood. You know how they talk Yiddish. He said he felt better among Jews. So, he marched with us. So anyway, we met Salek and Yaakov. So, whatever we had food, so we shared with them. We gave it to them. From the boxes. Over there was a bad camp. Was a camp no windows, no doors on the barracks. No concrete only dirt. We slept in the dirt. There was only a shell, four walls. There were window openings but no windows, no glass. There were doors, but no doors to close, just openings.

The final days of the war culminated with the constant shipment of Jews from one camp to another. Sometimes they stopped briefly at a camp and then immediately were shipped out to a different one. Dad saw heavy German artillery trains on the tracks. The Jews were not bothered by the planes. Rather, they felt good that the Germans were getting clobbered. And they knew that the war was coming to an end. During these forced train travels, there were train stops where the Jews saw high-ranking German officers. In a bizarre encounter, my dad recalled that the Nazi officers didn't have coffee, so they swapped their bread for the prisoners' coffee.

Dad had been at Ravensbück a few days before being shipped to Wöbbelin on April 16, his final concentration camp stop.

From Ravensbrück they shipped us to Ludwigslust then to Wöbbelin another camp more east.

The Jews of Europe were liberated in staggered fashion, depending on where in the war zone they happened to be. The Jews who were in the eastern arena were liberated earlier by the Russians. The Germans, knowing that the Russians were approaching, would, whenever possible, march or transport their Jewish cargo west. The marches caused thousands more Jewish deaths. Auschwitz had been liberated by the Russians in January 1945. The prisoners who were not gassed were marched out of Auschwitz before the liberators arrived. Many died or were shot dead on the march.

My sister and my sister-in-law were killed when they marched them out of Auschwitz.

Then there were Jews who were not marched but were transported in cattle cars, like my father and uncle. My father never understood the psychology behind the German decision to use trains to transport Jews rather than using them to transport German soldiers fleeing back to Germany.

Like the train transports of Jews at the war's end, there were other controls that the Nazis put in place that defy logic. The once a day "meal" was an example.

We had ½ hour for lunch. How do they feed 300 people in ½ hour? Everyone had to go into the hall at the same time and stand with his back to a bowl. Soup was in each bowl. At the signal everyone had to turn around at the same time and then we could eat.

Shortly after arriving at Wöbbelin, the inmates were forced into boxcars again. They were locked in the boxcars and were given no food or water. The prisoners didn't know what was going to happen.

Many years later, Dad came across a story about the prisoner filled trains that had departed Wöbbelin. The intent was to transport the prisoners to the port city of Lübeck, where they would be placed on ships on the Baltic. Before the train carrying my father was able to depart, the Americans cut off the rail line, effectively cancelling the ability of the Germans to continuing the transport of the Wöbbelin inmates. On May 3, 1945, the day after my dad was liberated, the English sank the three ships, killing the seven thousand inmates. Did the British purposely sink the ships so that they did not have to deal with the sick, filthy and hungry inmates? The documents are sealed for 100 years.

May 1, 1945

They left us in the train the whole night. One day they lined us up again and the train pulled in again, you know boxcars, and they put us on the train again. And sure enough, the locomotive came and stood there and we stayed there a whole night in the boxcars. The train didn't move.

May 2, 1945

The next day they let us out, but they didn't count us anymore. The Germans started to disappear. Usually they used to count us ... nobody should escape. We were a precious commodity. It's a joke. It's not a joke! It's the truth. Accountability. Dead or alive you gotta be there. Anyway, they let us out next day, but they didn't count us anymore. They let us back into the barracks. It had no floor, no windows. I was sick already. I was very sick. I had the diarrhea, that we got in the packages, I couldn't digest it. Because I wasn't used to cheese. I hadn't seen cheese in five years. And cheese is fat. And then we had other stuff like, everything was fat. Was good but not good for us. A lots of people got diarrhea and died. The Germans used to say that there are three ways to kill a Jew: shoot him, starve him, or give him a food package from America.

Around noon time we knew something was happening in the camp. I was told that the guards disappeared, the SS. Around noon, I don't exactly know the time, some inmates came and said some troops broke into the barbed wire. That was how I got the news. There we were liberated. I was too sick to get up and see who the liberators are. The Americans liberated us on May 2nd about noontime. My reaction was just we're liberated because I was too worn out to rejoice in this event, in this happening.

Throughout the war, my father made holes in his belt, the only remaining item he had from his pre-war life, to close around his thinning frame. Each hole is the evidence of the Nazis' ongoing starvation of my father over six years. The final hole on the belt is eighteen inches from the end. Some of the holes ripped the leather, mutilating it. Using the final hole as a reference, the diagonal of the belt is seven-and-a half inches. The last hole shows the circumference of the belt to be the size of my thigh.

Liberation

Dad, my Uncle Leon and the Baum brothers stayed the night, but nobody came to assist them. The next day, they left the camp and walked to Ludwigslust. En route to the town and as they went to look for food, they left my dad in a doorway because he was too weak to walk. A German woman opened the door. Dad was wearing stripes so the woman knew he was from the camps. Dad said the woman was scared. She gave dad a pair of military pants.

My dad talks about his liberation.

The Germans just left. We always thought the liberation was going to be excitement. But when the liberation came it was just another day. Another thing, before liberation we used to get a little food. After liberation there was no food. No one gave us food. Someone said that soon we would be rescued and taken care of. A day passed and no one came. Thank goodness my brother Leon was in better shape than I was. I was in really bad shape. I could hardly walk. We waited for help to come, but none came. So, my brother, the two Baum brothers and I decided to go off on our own. Leon, the Baum brothers and I walked out of the camp on our own. Nobody helped us. Later we heard that no one came to help the prisoners. Thousands of Jews died just waiting. They died in filth. People just lying and dying in filth. The Americans didn't do anything for us. If you didn't go out and get food, you didn't eat. It wasn't organized. I remember, the first day I didn't go out. The rumor was that the Americans were going to send in ambulances and medical help and help us. And food. We decided that we'll wait and see what will develop. A whole day, no one came. We still slept in the dirt. So next day, we decided we would go to Ludwiglust, the next town. We didn't eat. We didn't have any food. I remember I couldn't lift my foot. I had to use my hands to lift it or go around something. There was a small log along the way. I couldn't lift my leg to walk over it. I had to walk around it. I had a concentration camp jacket and a blanket over my head. I was standing in a doorway. A woman opened the door and handed me a pair of German soldier's pants. She didn't offer me any food or nothing. Finally, Leon, Salik and Yaakov came back. They brought me one cookie and said they found a place to stay. Nobody came to our help. It started to rain.

My uncle and the Baums found a washroom/laundry room on the first floor of a house. Somewhere, they found mattresses to put on the floor. They didn't bother the family that lived upstairs in the house.

We walked into a house, into the laundry room. It had a stove and a place for us to sleep on the floor. We stayed in the laundry room. We could have gone into the house and kick the Germans out but we didn't do it. The Germans were afraid. They hid in the attic. But we didn't do anything. The big heroes hiding in the attic sent their ambassador to smell out what's going in the little laundry room. You know who they sent—the grandmother. I never met the rest of the family. I lied down on the floor. I was tired and sick. I had diarrhea. She asked why I was laying on the floor. Leon told her I had diarrhea. The old lady brought some liquid and slowly the diarrhea went away. I never saw anybody else. I know there was a daughter. They never came.

Uncle Leon worked in an American kitchen where he used to get cans of food. They got parts of the chicken that the Americans would not eat. Dad was the cook for the four of them. Gradually, he recuperated.

I used to get up in the middle of the night to eat and go back to sleep.

About two weeks after they arrived, while Dad was home alone, the door burst open and an American soldier walked in with a German interpreter. They told Dad to go outside.

The American soldier brought Dad to a camp where there were hundreds of thousands of people milling around. There were prisoners of war, forced laborers, Jewish prisoners, families, criminals, single people, people from different countries and ethnic groups.

Outside was a jeep with a little trailer. The Americans had jeeps and trailers. They imposed a curfew and they went from house to house to seek out foreigners. They walked in and they put me into that little trailer. I didn't know where they were taking me. I wasn't really scared. I was just bewildered because I didn't know what was going on. Here I was sick, I could hardly walk, recuperating and they took us to a former German air force base. The front gate was manned by American soldiers. And they drove us in. They let us go. There were there a lots of foreign people, you know from Europe. They were from Poland, Germany, Yugoslavia, you name it, and everybody had a different spot. And apparently from there they used to drive them by truck to the border. The Russians were there about a couple kilometers. And then the Russians took it over. And everybody went to their own country of origin. So I was by myself there and I want to get out. But you had a guard in the front of the gate and he didn't let you out. As I was walking around, I met some, former concentration camp inmates, Jewish guys. I met Salek there. They took him too from some other place. There were Polish prisoners and I went over and I talked to them. I said how can I get out from this camp? They told me over there is a gate. You see, the Americans were guarding the front gate, but they were not guarding the perimeter. We walked out from the camp. We walked back to the city. But we didn't know there was a curfew. So, we walked a distance and the Americans took us back into custody and they took us back into camp. So as we walkin we met a whole group and there was one guy he knew English and he said, "You know what, when we get to the gate don't speak Polish, speak German and they'll ask us what nationality you say German Jews." So, as we got to the gate, and the American officer ask, "What nationality?" and we said German Jews, in German "deutshe Juden." He said, "German Jews? There's no room for German Jews here. You don't belong here." And they made us leave. That was I guess the third time. Three times walking back and forth. The second time we just snuck out, walked here walked out there. So we walked back to the city and they stopped us, because the curfew an American officer I guess he was. And we said German Jews. And he said you get in the backyard here and wait til 5 o'clock. Five o'clock the curfew's gonna be over and you can go home. And then 5 o'clock the curfew was over and we walked out. In the backyard there were more Germans they were sitting there. They waited for the curfew to pass too. But I didn't know where I lived. You know, I never left the place and here is a city and I have to go back but I didn't know exactly where it is. But I knew it wasn't far from the railroad station.

Dad was not with Salek. They had separated at some point and Dad did not remember the details. Somehow, Dad was able to find the house. Uncle Leo was working in the American kitchen and happened not to be taken to the repatriation area as Dad was. They stayed in Ludwigslust about five weeks. Foreigners had started leaving the city and the Russians were getting ready to take it over.

Dad recuperated enough to travel. So, Dad, Uncle Leo and the Baums went to the repatriation area. They found it to be almost deserted. Most of the foreigners had been sent to their country of origin. The Americans had also left, replaced by the English army. Instead of sending them east back to Poland, they sent them west because there were no longer transports going east. Moreover, Polish Jews were no longer forced to go back. Two months later, they were told that they had to move to the English controlled town of Lüneburg. My dad, Uncle Leo, and the Baums were trucked into Lüneburg, where they were greeted by English soldiers. There the English army had set aside buildings for prisoners of war. They were the only Jews there. However, there were other army camps in the area where Jewish survivors were staying. The brothers left the camp and went to reside in the part of the city where a Jewish community center had been established.

The English zone was well organized to meet the needs of the survivors. For the first time in five years, and much to their surprise, they were treated with human decency. The soldiers helped my father and uncle take their meager belongings off the truck. My dad stayed with the knapsacks as the others followed the English soldiers into a four-story barrack. They had been told to take their belongings and go to the first floor. When they got there, they were given a yellow card and told to enter. After entering, they were told they should take their belongings and go to the second floor. On the second floor they were given another yellow card. When they entered, the officer in charge told them they were on the wrong floor and told them to go to the third floor. When they got to the third floor, again they were given a yellow card. Upon entering that floor, the soldier in charge told them to go to the fourth floor, where they were once again given a yellow card. The fourth floor of that barrack would be their home, along with other eastern European refugees, for the next few weeks.

My father, uncle and the Baums soon learned that the yellow cards entitled them to eat their meals in a special mess hall set up for the refugees. Food was served in chow lines where Germans put food on each tray. Dad said the meals were great—the first real meals they had had in six years. Each yellow card allowed the holder entry into the dining hall. Each card had tabs that were removed when one went to eat.

Nobody was telling me anything. They told you get on the truck, you got on the truck. They put together a convoy of trucks and they took us over the Elbe and the Elbe was the west Germany and we landed in the English zone. We had it very good in the English camp. When we got there, we got off the truck. And all three went to explore, into the building. I waited; I watched the knapsacks. You know food we carried. So, nobody should steal it. And they came back and they said, 'Okay we'll go into the building.' But they brought cards with them. What were the cards, we didn't know. When they went in, apparently, into the building, they gave 'em a card with four coupons. They issued breakfast, lunch, tea and crumpets or whatever and then dinner. But when they went in by the time they walked out they had four cards each one. And you got six cigarettes a day. Each floor they went, they were given a card, they went over and they asked for a card. So, they wind up with four cards, each one of us had four cards. By the time we got to the third floor, we were supposed to stay on the third floor, but third floor married couples were staying. Single people were supposed to live in the attic. So, when we got to the attic they were handing out cards for the single people. So, we wound up with four cards each one and so we could have four breakfasts, four lunches, four dinners. When you passed through the chow line in the evening, they took away the last coupon and they gave you a new card for the next day. So, you went through the line for lunch, you went breakfast so you went two times, four times, three times but you didn't eat the bread, you know, the bread you could save. So, it was white bread, good bread, and we used to have, by the end of the day, we had a loaf of bread. And this we eat nighttime. We ate in the middle of the night. And at that time, we met already a few survivors. And they lived in the camp too. It was growing slowly.

One day they were walking in Lüneburg when they saw three young Jewish women, survivors as well. But Dad said something was odd. It turned out that because they were German citizens, they were given ration cards just like the rest of the German population, which meant that they were living on a very meager diet. Dad, Uncle Leo and the Baums suggested that the women come with them. They took them to the camp and told the English commander that they found cousins. So, the women were issued cards and came from their apartment in the city to eat at the camp. They did the same for four Jewish Hungarian women they met.

Dad stayed at the camp six months before the English closed it. While living in the city for a few months, Dad and the others learned of entitlements available to them. They were entitled to a room in the city and financial aid. Uncle Leo and Dad were assigned a room with the Neumanns, a childless couple about 60 years old, where they would live for five years. An office, set up for concentration camp survivors, gave them money for living expenses. They paid the Neumanns rent. They also helped the Neumanns out by giving them food. I asked Dad if the Neumanns knew about the atrocities. He told me the story about a train with prisoners that was passing through Lüneburg when it was bombed. The train's prisoners ran from the train into the city. The German residents helped the SS round up the prisoners and then watched them massacre them.

At the end of the war, the English forced the Germans to witness the opening of a mass grave. In order to receive a ration card, Germans had to be at the gravesite when it was opened.

In 1945 they opened the grave. They dug 'em out. They made all the Germans march by and look at them, the grave. The English made sure that all the Germans, they didn't get the ration card it had to be stamped or something like this. And they buried each corpse individually. They were mostly non-Jews but there were Jews too. I have pictures of this place. And every year we used to go and have services there.

The lucky Jews were those who survived with a family member or who were able to track down any surviving family member. Throughout Europe, survivors sought leads and information about a mother, father, sister, brother, and other family. My father learned, from Meyer's wife's sister, Fela, who had survived Auschwitz and the death march to Bergen-Belsen, about his sister's Leah's demise. Fela had witnessed the shooting of Leah, during the death march. She had fallen, so a German soldier murdered her.

Of the 10 percent of European Jewry that managed to survive, most were left either alone or with one other surviving family member. They were desperate to start their lives anew. This led to pairings. While in Germany, many survivors married others who had survived. Jews thrown together from all parts of Europe were meeting, mingling and marrying. A miniscule number wished to return to their country of origin.

We all married Jewish spouses. A few married non-Jewish. Very few Jews stayed in Germany. They went all over the world—Canada, Australia, South America. But nobody went back to Poland. Lola and Franka's brother, Lolick, went back to Poland. Idealists to rebuild Poland. But he went back and became a gynecologist. He married a German girl and had children. Gomulka kicked out the Jews in the 1950s-60s. The Poles concocted a story to entice him to leave. They said they would charge him with experimenting on a Polish woman. So he left and went to Sweden. But the Swedes sent the Jewish doctors to northern Sweden to work for three years before they would be allowed to work in a southern city like Stockholm. The idealists wanted me to go too. I told them I'd come back after they finished rebuilding Poland.

Five years later, my father left Germany for the United States.

The Need for Emotional Containment

Dad considered this taping of his experiences as a summary of events. I pressed him to tell me how he felt. He started to get irritated with me.

A tape of a conversation, this is a report, more like a summary. But if you go into detail it's very hard to, to, to express a self accurately. What you felt from the first minute the Germans came in, the terror that you felt inside and then the happenings, day to day terror and then you have, how do you describe the hunger? The the the way they treated, the rumors, the the happenings, you know, people went, "They did here and they did here." And and you were scared. You didn't know what's going to happen to you next day. How do you describe the suffering from thousands of people at the same time? How? How do I describe it to you? I'm not a Tolstoy. Like you see, if we were in the ghetto, can I describe, just if somebody would had the literary genius and to put to words just how people were get into the ghetto. When the final order came all the Jews had to go in the ghetto. If you woulda stand you woulda watched all the haggard, the old, the sick, the young, the kids; they were schlepping on on on, all their belongings had to fit into a little baby carriage. Or a little wagon, or the rushka, it's a tiaka. It's hard to describe the mass of people walking from the city into the ghetto and dragging all this little belongings with no, the faces, the scared faces and getting in the ghetto with no hope and they didn't know what's gonna happen to them. Can you describe each one individually? It was a tragedy of mass proportion. And then in the ghetto, you were in the ghetto, you had those constant demand of people being shipped out of the ghetto under all kind of pretenses: for work, there too many Jews together gonna ship 'em here, send 'em to work. You never found out what happened to them. Like first they came in and took out all the people they were in... you know we had a hospital and then we had for mentally sick people. They were not really mentally sick they were mentally but they were not dangerous people. They came in, one morning, and they took 'em out to be killed. And then one, two escaped and they forced them, the Jewish administration, to go and find them and bring 'em so they can ship 'em out otherwise they're going to be retribution, you know, they'll take out 10, or a hundred of healthy Jews. And then you worked and the hunger, the constant hunger. And you had the shperre, the curfews. They used to take the older people, the kids, the sick people. All kind of excuses they had. That lasted for four days sometimes, a week. The feeling in your stomach, you had knot in your stomach that didn't wanna go away. You didn't know where to hide and what to hide and you don't know what's gonna happen next day and so far and where you gonna and this was goin on constant. How do you describe it? The constant hunger. Constant, constant hunger, day after day after day. The winter, cold in the winter. Then you trapped. You, nowhere to go. No help, no help in sight, absolutely. You were isolated from the world, from any world, from the Jewish world. Nobody bothered with you. You were like, anybody puts you in a room, throws away the key and you sit there. And you're at the mercy of the jailer. He want, he gives you food as much as he wants he gives you. He don't want, he don't give you. Do something about it. Right? So how can you describe it? It's hard! And that goes on day after day, and year after year. You watch constantly whole families that lived in the house disappearing. New families moving in. You don't even know who they are. Whole families disappearing. And you never heard from them anymore. And then when you got to Auschwitz, the, if any can describe hell, that was Auschwitz. All of a sudden, they throw you into Auschwitz, that terrible treatment that you got. It's hard to describe so vividly, so accurately…. It was terrible! It was awful! You know you were nothing. You were constantly hussled, and pushed, and they used to make the appels, and used to make exercises, you never knew what's gonna be, who's gonna be taken out and beaten and whatever. You just existed. You weren't the master of yourself. You don't know what's gonna happen the next day or next minute. In Auschwitz you didn't have anything. Four hundred people, I don't know how many people slept in one barrack on the floor. There was pushing and shoving and beating. And the appel used to line us up in the morning, wake up in the morning, four o'clock in the morning and everything was pushing and shoving and beating. But the mental, what you were thinking. And then across you had Birkenau, the crematorium, you know, the gas chambers. It was really hell on earth (Dad sits silently thinking).

Dad tells me about hunger.

You have to be very disciplined so that you don't get violent. You have to have a lot of self-control. The hunger pains are constant. Only at the very end of the war, did the hunger pains stop. I didn't feel any more hunger. When they brought the Red Cross packages, I didn't care.

I ask Dad if there was a smell.

I'll tell you Marilyn, I was so insensitive to anything. I didn't feel anything, I didn't smell anything, I didn't do anything. I just existed. You couldn't sleep nights. I remember they let us sometimes between breakfast and lunch, you could roam around. I used to lay down on the ground and and I used to sleep. Because at nights you couldn't sleep. There were so many people on the ground, one next to other. You never knew, who, who was, it was, have you ever seen cattle drive, so many pushed to together and driven in one job? More or less like it was. It was sheer terror (Dad sits quietly in his own thoughts). *And I then was lucky. I was only in nine days or eight days in Auschwitz. And I was lucky to get out. But even so, we got out but there was no picnic. People died in the camps they shipped us to. Most of 'em died.*

I ask Dad what it was like seeing people die around him all the time.

You're insensitive. You don't, you don't, you build up a resistance. It's a dead person and you go on living. It's part of the survival. You couldn't get emotional. It didn't have to affect you. If it affected you, if you got the notion, I will not survive, you know because of this, then you didn't survive. You see, in your mind you didn't wait whether you will survive or you won't

64

survive. It was to live another day and the war is going on and maybe you'll survive. If you lived with this idea, you had a good chance to live longer. If you gave up, you said, no use, then you had less of a chance of survival.

I ask Dad about surviving all those years.

You had to be very persistent.

I ask Dad how a person copes with such personal tragedies.

The minute when we were liberated, we were new people. A new life. You couldn't live the past. The past is gone and we had to start building from new. We did not forget what happened, but we had to start a new life, start building again.

I ask my dad how one puts the past away.

It's hard to explain. The past was terrible, terrible. So in order to function, in your brain you divide it. You divide the past, that was one thing. And then you start a new chapter, the future.

I ask my dad if the past creeps up on him.

All the time. All the time. All the time. When you sit you think about it, about events. What was going on: the hunger, deportations. It's visual, you can see it. Names and people, friends, and conversations. All those things. It does not disappear. It's like you have a library. You have a book about this and that's another book. In our mind, the past is one book, one chapter the future started it's a new chapter. When we got out, the survivors, we were realists. We were realistic. We couldn't bring back the past, the families. And here starts something new that you can start a new life from the beginning and build a new life under tradition and whatever you learned and start a new life and build families and get back to normal.

I comment that I would have found it nearly impossible to go on after losing my whole family.

If anybody would have told me I would have say, 'It's terrible.' But when you live something, it changes. You become a different person. The attitude change.

I ask how his attitude changed.

It was a tragedy. People treat us so terrible. But we should we should not succumb. We have to fight back. The only thing to fight back was to start a new life. What would it do? After all this that we lived through to just give up, wouldn't have served no purpose. You see we didn't go after the war to psychiatrists, psychologists. There were no psychiatrists, no psychologists. We realized what happened it won't come back. All the things it won't come back. And all the things will not come back. We were aware of it. But it shouldn't take the better part of us. The past is still with us. I remember my brothers, my sisters. I remember even how they looked like. I remember my brother, when the SS man after he gave him the salt to drink and my brother became delirious. I remember it. But what could I do? The question is what do you do? What do you do? You commit suicide? What do you do?

My dad is clearly upset with the memories.

The war was over, we got outta camp, started a new chapter and we took advantage of it. We took advantage of the better part, we are free. And we can start all over again.

I ask my dad what he thinks about when he thinks about his parents.

My parents they were very nice. My father was a hardworking man. He was very honest. He had his stresses and problems to take care of a family of nine. Living conditions were different. And I could picture myself my father how he felt when the war started and he was helpless. Here was a provider, and the war started, and that goes for all the Jewish families, all the Jewish fathers, how helpless he was and what was going through his mind. I was a young kid. I didn't realize because I didn't have to take care on anybody. I was taken care. I was 15 years old. You're still home. Someone's gonna take care on you. Everything is provided for you. Now I can think like my father was thinking in that time. Because they were despaired and there's nothing much they could do for us. They couldn't get us food because they didn't have themself. They did everything they could. My mother felt terrible. Here she was a balabusta [an exemplary homemaker]. She used to cook for us and see that everybody is fed in the right time and had good and dressed and had warm in the winter, had warm clothes, and here you come and you can't do a thing. You can't do a thing. They must have felt horrible. Right? There was not much they could'a do for us. It was a tragedy, an ongoing tragedy. Just like you take a bunch of people and you put them in a prison and you guard'em. You become helpless.

My mom had wanted to immigrate to Israel. My dad wanted to come to the United States. My dad had his way. However, getting into the U.S. was difficult with the continued quotas. My mother's sister, Yanka, had immigrated to Canada and petitioned for my parents to join her and her husband. They were approved. Before they were set to leave for Canada, a relative of my dad had agreed to take responsibility for my parents if they came to the United States. They were approved.

I had some family that immigrated to the United States before the war. We notified them by letter that we were coming to New York. We thought they would give us some assistance which it turned out not to be the case. We were taken from the airport to Grand Central or Penn Station. I thought that my family would come and take care of us. We were sitting there and no one came.

The Great Crime

This is the story why you may regret,
If ever your memory should let you forget,
How nations coerced were made to obey,
By one man's cruel mind, one astray.
For unless you painfully, carefully heed,
History's lesson may be wasted, indeed.

Still stood the air on dark September,
Etched in the memories of those who remember,
Black clouds suspended, in their breath
Carried forebodings praising death,
And when the world from slumber awoke,
Late was the hour, madness amok.

From high above skies arose a thunder,
Scattering fire down way yonder,
Strewing flames and dust to the east and west,
Echoing deep cries from the mountain crests.
With blazing torches across Europe's plains,
The German armies spread over wide terrains.

Blight and destruction they sowed everywhere,
Encircling free nations trapped in a snare;
Through verdant valleys their armies have trod,
No boundaries, no realms-with no fear of God.
Behind the shadows of this and destruction,
Stood one maniac's ambitions of world reconstruction.

My tongue the name he has born shall skip,
For fear it may mar and disgrace my lip;
With poisonous wrath his breath infected,
Like fire from a mouth of a dragon ejected.
The man possessed by purity of race,
Jews from this earth has pledged to efface.

While his fist went up in furious guests,
He cried: "Let's rid the world of pests."
The German people praised his great devise,

68

They thought it a noble and wise enterprise.
Like demons in black shirts their bodies arrayed,
Haughty, disdainful, dark death they conveyed.

By his side they stood in an endless throng;
Seemingly ordinary people-millions strong
Yet people who willfully, without warning,
Straight from the altar on a Sunday morning,
With uncontrollable enmity and aggression,
Brutally murdered with a killer's passion.

What fools, so void of sight with blighted souls,
As to obey a man so merciless and foul
Whose one desire, just to please his whim,
Deprived humanity of dignity and esteem;
His mighty crown though threatened by a few-
Yet threatened by a defenseless, unarmed Jew?

O mocker, o travesty of glorious bravery?
To yoke a man and throw him into slavery,
Then, like a devil's monstrous, sinister game,
To feast your eyes upon his misery and shame;
And to his self-dug grave to cast the prey,
Whenever your eyes no more avail of play!

Too wearisome the chore for "Herrenfolk" so noble,
The blood, decay-why go through so much trouble?
When with much more proficient skill,
One can bring thousand lives to still.
One knob to turn and odorless and deathly gas,
Would bring their miserable, wretched forms to pass.

There are the chimneys dark and dusty gray,
From which last hopes have fled and smoked away;
Gas chambers with hermetically closed doors,
And human ashes strewn upon the floors.
The names unknown, erased, from earth effaced-
And not a sign the graves above to grace.

There are the children innocent of evil scheme,

And mothers brutally torn away from them;
The old, the sages forward bent with age,
The fathers, brothers, sisters cut down with outrage.
A throng of shadows left behind the walls-
A breathless image of six million souls.

Tell me, you sages in this earthly sphere-
For cry of justice, or for human care!
What punishment deserves a crime so dire?
Perhaps the doom that quenched their own desire?
To strike the core in their devastation,
As they have pierced the hearts of our nation.

The peace came back and guns were stilled again,
And home returned the battle-worn men.
No monuments, no medals breasts adorn,
Of those who died in life's early morn.
For the six million killed the peace but brought no morrow,
For those remained just weeping hearts and sorrow.

"The Great Crime," by Anna Geslewitz

Anna's Story

Parents and Siblings of Anna Geslewitz

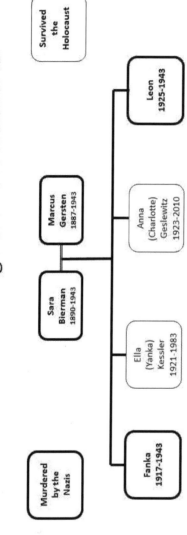

Survived the Holocaust

Murdered by the Nazis

Marcus Gersten
1887-1943

Sara Bierman
1890-1943

Fanka
1917-1943

Ella
(Yanka)
Kessler
1921-1983

Anna
(Charlotte)
Geslewitz
1923-2010

Leon
1925-1943

My mother was an intelligent, shy, quiet, and unassuming woman. She avoided confrontations at all costs and never raised her voice. She used to say that she could not yell. She never forced her viewpoint on anyone and preferred to avoid controversy. She was a gentle soul who had difficulty verbalizing her feelings and emotions. My mother had a beautiful singing voice and was a poet. She was accepted to medical school in Germany after the war but turned it down to come to America. My mother, I like to say, was understated.

My mother met my father in Germany after the war. He was a good-looking young man. My mother said that she liked him because he was outgoing and liked to talk. This way, he would do the talking and she did not have to. On the darker side, my father exerted tremendous control over her. She found it easier to give into him than to argue and risk his temper flaring. This she tried to avoid at all costs but was not successful. My father's volatile temper reared its ugly head a few times a week. He never hit my mom, but he would find ways to verbally humiliate her. When I spoke up in her defense, he would blame her for allowing me to talk back to him. She would then tell me to be quiet.

Soon after my youngest sister, Phyllis, was born my mother became extremely depressed. I don't know if it was due to postpartum depression, having three children under the age of five, the trauma of the war or my father's volatility; perhaps it was all combined. She went to see a doctor. According to my mother, he told her she needed to snap out of it because she had three young children to take care of. What he said rang true, she told me, so she snapped out of it. However, later in life, she again complained of feeling depressed. My sisters and I urged her to see someone about it. We made an appointment with a psychiatrist. When my father heard about it, he convinced her not to go. He did not believe in psychiatrists or psychologists. Yet, my parents stayed together for 62 years. My mother died on December 14, 2010. My father died two months later on February 19, 2011.

The Family

I was born Charlotte Gersten in Lwow, Poland in 1923. I was only eighteen when the Germans invaded eastern Poland. My family consisted of my parents. I had an oldest sister who was about seven years older than I [Fanny, Fanka]. And Auntie Yanka. Her actual name was Lucia. And then I had a younger brother who was about two years younger than me. His name was Lonek. Actually, here you would call him Leo. My oldest sister was born in Budapest, Hungary. During WWI they (my mother's parents) went to Budapest. Maybe my father wanted to avoid the draft. After the war they came back to Poland.

My father was tall, about six feet. When he was young, he must've been very good looking. He had dark hair and blue eyes. He wore glasses because when he was a young man, he was repairing watches and he had an accident and something fell in his eye. And in those days, they couldn't save his eye so he had one glass eye.

My mother was maybe a little bit taller than I am. (My mother was five feet tall.). I don't even know if she was an inch taller than I. But my mother had a very cute figure. Later, she got a little bit heavy. I remember she used to go on a diet even in those days. But she had dark hair and since I remember her hair was always mixed with gray. She had brown eyes. And I don't know, none of us kids got her nose because she had a straight pointy nose.

As was typical of their day, my grandparents met through a matchmaker.

You know in those days everybody was introduced. It wasn't like now you fall in love and you get married. They had a matchmaker and the matchmaker brought the girl and brought the guy together. And if they, well most of the time, the marriages were even arranged before. But this wasn't the case with my parents. My parents there was just a matchmaker and he brought them together. And my father looked at my mother, my father was a very good-looking man. My mother, I don't think she was this good looking. She was kind of short, my father was tall. And it was funny because she (Aunt Esther) always used to tell me how they met. She said they got together and he looked at my mother and they asked him whether he liked her and said, "It's a girl. What's the difference? It's a girl." (Mom laughs.) And I guess he must have liked her because otherwise, I don't know (laughing). I don't even know whether they asked my mother if she likes him (laughing).

Because my mother's family was well off, they were able to afford many things that were beyond the reach of the average Polish family.

We were considered pretty rich before the war. We had better food. We used to have a nanny, an old Polish woman, in the house because my mother was in the store. To go to movies was no problem for me. There were people who were richer, who had more. There were people even who had cars! Like, we had a telephone. There weren't too many people who did. My father used to call Switzerland. He had to call abroad because this was the main source for his store. I guess in comparison to other people, we were pretty well off. Our apartment was beautiful. It was big. It already had the bathroom and the bathtub in the house. It was expensive to keep a big apartment like this. It was one, two, three, four, five, six rooms, like six bedrooms. My father had a jewelry store and he was selling wholesale and retail. He supplied furniture for watches, parts, parts for watches; it was called in Polish "furniture." They were coming all around from the small towns, to my father, to buy those parts for watches. Our store was on the second floor, together with the apartment. A part of our apartment was actually a store. One room was the store. We had like an entrance hall. They (customers) just went through the entrance hall to the store. Downstairs were mostly stores. There were no families living downstairs. See, it was a completely different setup than here. Here, the residential areas don't have stores, unless like maybe the big cities like in Brooklyn. Where we lived there was on the corner a drugstore and then people lived upstairs. My father didn't have a storefront. My father didn't need a storefront because we were pretty well known all around and it's like here you see a wholesale place. We didn't need the advertising.

My parents spoke Yiddish among themselves but never with us. I understood every word but I never spoke. With us, they only spoke Polish. Just like I spoke to you only English and with Daddy, in the beginning, I spoke Polish. I learned more Jewish (Yiddish) when I married Daddy because he spoke a lot of Jewish. It isn't that I learned. I understood everything but I was just not used to speaking the language.

As my grandfather's business prospered, the family was able to move to a nicer neighborhood in the center of the city.

From Zhudlana [street name], we moved to Krakowska. I remember even the number. Krakowska 14. It was about a block away from, they called it Wielke Rinek, Nowe Rinek or Wielke Rinek. I don't remember. It was like a center. It was a marketplace. The street that we lived on was a pretty commercial street. There were stores all along the street, on the first floor, and people lived upstairs. I'll tell you, not only that we didn't know any non-Jewish people, I tell you the truth, we lived in this big house, we didn't know anybody from the neighbors. You know when we first met them? When they had the air raids during war, when the war started. And we had to go to the basement, we met the neighbors.

My mother's family was able to afford to send their children to a Jewish high school. Except for a token number of Jewish students, Jews were not allowed to enter the state high schools. Had the war not broken out, my mother would have gone on to study at the university level. Catholic, but not Jewish Poles, were allowed into the public high schools. Jewish children went to private high schools if their parents could afford the tuition.

The Polish education authorities were able to weed out of contention the Jewish students by their names or if they looked Jewish. The likelihood of a Jewish student slipping through the discriminatory public education system was slim. Additionally, pervasive anti-Semitism prevented most Jewish Poles from working in government agencies. Since the children of government officials were given education privileges, like high school, the vast majority of Jewish students were automatically barred from higher education public schools. A Jewish student had to be exceptional to be given a public high school education. The child of a government official did not have to be an exemplary student.

We were better educated. We had high school education. High school education in Poland was like here college. Compulsory was only seventh grade. And from there on you had to pay your way. It was called gymnasium [the "g" like in "get"] which is here high school. And they were private. There were, there were some state schools, gymnasiums, but for a Jew to get into this school you really had to be a son or daughter of a government worker, and how many government workers were Jewish?

My mother lived in a predominantly Jewish neighborhood. Generally, the Catholic and Jewish children went to separate elementary public schools. The exception was if a Jewish child lived in a predominantly Catholic neighborhood and there were no Jewish schools in the area. Only Jewish students attended the private Jewish schools. There they were taught the secular curriculum as well as Hebrew and religion. If separated educationally, there was little chance that Catholic and Jewish children would socialize. My mother had no neighborhood Christian friends.

I went to a high school where there were only Jewish children. It was a private high school. I never even applied [to non-Jewish high school]. It never occurred to me to apply. You know, nobody, no Jewish person would apply to a state school unless they were children of government workers. When we were little we lived in a pretty Jewish section. There were not all Jews but there were Jewish sections, more, I would say, percent Jewish. Even the state schools there were for Jewish children and not Jewish children. Of course, if you lived in a district where there weren't enough Jews you went with non-Jews. I'll tell you the truth, Jewish parents liked to send the children to the schools where there were only Jewish children. The non-Jewish children were usually bothering the kids. They were beating them up. They were calling them names. It was just easier for a Jewish child to be in a Jewish school.

I don't ever remember having a non-Jewish friend throughout high school. I didn't know any. See, like Irka [my mother's friend, who we knew in New Jersey, grew up in Krakow] *used to have non-Jewish friends. The suburbs weren't like the suburbs here. She lived in the suburbs of Krakow. And they were mixed there so she had non-Jewish friends. In the city, there were very very few Jewish children associating with non-Jews. I had friends in high school who lived not far from where they went to school. So, I have no idea if they associated with non-Jews. Mostly they associated with wherever they went to school.*

I had friends. But my friends, they lived, not even in the neighborhood. I used to walk to see them. They were school friends. Regina Folk, we used to call her Figa, was my best friend in high school. I guess Rachela Korb was my best friend in elementary school until she went to Israel. Her family moved to Israel before the war. I wanted to go to Israel so badly after she left! But I guess it didn't work out. The name of my elementary school was Czackiego. The name of the high school was Kammerling. Frieda Feiertag was another best friend.

Figa was little like a dried-out fig. That's why we used to call her Figa. She was short and skinny, shorter than I was. She was very bright. One of the brightest kids in class. Her father was a butcher and her mother used to help him out in the store. They lived upstairs from the butcher shop. Her father was such a yucky guy. When he sat down to eat, no matter who was in the house, he burped and farted. They had a maid in the house. She used to make dirty jokes. I remember accountants used to come to their house. We didn't let them do their work. We used to walk in and bother them. We were stupid teenagers. I used to sing, I had a very good voice. When the movies from the United States came to Poland we used to go and watch them. After those movies we went to Figa's house and instead of doing homework, we were dancing and singing. Do you know, people used to stand outside and listen.

Generally, students entered high school in sixth grade. Since my mother entered a year later, in seventh grade, she had to take a proficiency exam that she passed. Entering a year later saved my mom's parents one year's tuition.

I remember, I learned in five weeks, I made up, for a whole year. It's not only arithmetic, Polish, history, geography; but they had German and Latin in high school which they didn't have in grade school. So, I made up in five weeks what they learned in a whole year. I finished high school. There were four years of high school. But because I went to the second [skipping the first year of high school by taking the exams], *I had three years of high school and two years lyceum. So, it's altogether five years.*

Bigotry and the harassment of Jews, children and adults, were frequent. It was not uncommon for public officials to visit Jewish businesses looking for ways trump up charges against the business. The idea behind the visits was to extract bribes, which the Jewish businessmen had to pay. The lives, of Jewish children among the Catholic children, were difficult as well. The Catholic boys used to come in gangs to bully the Jewish children.

We had a nice family life. We were very close knit. It was wonderful. It was great. But, they (the Poles) didn't let us live. *Before the war, you were persecuted. If Jewish people had a store, the government put taxes on them, all kinds of taxes. It was draining them.*

They [government agents] *used to come to the store and they used to look and they used to search. I remember they used to make searches. I don't know what they were looking for. And they* [Jewish store owners] *had to pay them off. There were a lot of grafts going on.*

I remember when we used to come out from school, they used to harass, used to call names, used to beat up. ZHID, ZHID, ZHID. HALAMED ZHID. [Zhid was the deragotory term for someone Jewish]

Most European Jews kept Kosher and observed the Sabbath. They were, in contemporary terms, Orthodox Jews.

There was no such thing like conservative or reformed. There were only orthodox. The only shuls [synagogues] *were orthodox. My mother kept kosher. My mother was religious. My father was observant and used to go Friday and Saturday to synagogue, but my mother was religious, observant. She didn't ask any questions. And my father asked questions. My father was very learned in Jewish. But he liked to discuss it.*

Saturdays I used to get together with my friends. When we were very little, my parents used to take us for a walk. My father's youngest brother, Simcha, had a very nice store, a jewelry store in a fancy area. We used to go Saturday to visit. Simcha used to take us out to buy chocolate. His wife that he married was college educated. I remember, she was tall and her mouth always puckered. They had two children. This was not long before the war. They were all killed.

My maternal great grandmother's name was Bierman. When my mother and her siblings were young, they used to spend summers with their maternal grandparents.

My mother's parents lived in Chorosnica, Poland. It was a small village. You know my grandfather was a farmer. So, he had horses and chickens and a dog. My parents used to bring us to my grandparents. We used to stay there for the whole summer. My cousin from Sweden, she lived with our grandparents in the same house in the village. (My mother's cousin, Tsila, immigrated to Sweden after the war). *Her last name was Bierman. She was the daughter of my mother's brother. Later, when we became teenagers, we wouldn't go anymore. We wanted to stay in the city. We were bored there. There really wasn't much to do. My mother had a sister living not far from the village. Her name was Mincha Hoch. We used to walk, my brother and sisters, to my aunt's house. My aunt had two boys and one girl. Never would you recognize that this girl was Jewish. She was heavy. She had blue eyes and blond hair and her nose was straight. She had no Jewish features. They took her family away. She escaped on Christian papers. And then my mother had another sister, Yetta. She was not married. But in the adjoining village there was a guy who was in love with her. She didn't want him. I saw him after the war. He survived with his wife and two kids.*

The Polaks were dirty, even though they used to call Jews dirty Jews. They used to have some kind of an itch between their fingers because they were dirty. My grandma used to make salve for the condition between their fingers, in exchange for butter. It was itching and contagious too.

My mother's family was not close to her father's family. She met her father's parents, who lived in a small town, only once. My paternal great grandparents had three sons and two daughters. The oldest, Shiya, immigrated to the United States after WWI. He married and had eleven children. Another brother immigrated to Vienna before the war. Of the two sisters, Esther survived and Sarah perished during the war. Esther was an astute businesswoman.

Esther had like a department store on a small scale. And we went to visit her. And she had a maid and she had a big house already then. She was the one who really was the business head. She was a pretty wealthy woman. Her husband was a very nice man, but he didn't have a business head. He used to help her. Esther, she survived. Milek and Zosha were her children. She was hidden with Milek and Zosha all the time throughout the war. And then my father had a younger sister, Sarah, living in Lwow. When she was getting married everyone contributed, all the brothers and sisters, contributed to the naden [dowry]. He [her husband] was a poor guy. In order for him to support her and the family, they opened a booth and they were selling leather. They also had two children. They also perished.

A common theme in my mother's reminiscences was the rampant anti-Semitism that surrounded the Jews. It was of no use for the Jews to complain to the police since the police force was made up men who, like the general population, were anti-Semitic.

You were not allowed to do, to go wherever you wanted to go, to do whatever you wanted to do. I remember we could never go to a certain park which was on the other side of town. It was a beautiful park, but they were chasing the Jews out of there. The students! Polish teenagers! They were beating them [Jews] up. Jews didn't want to have fights with them. Because they could have never won. No matter what. The police would have been always on their [Catholics'] side. Because they're Jew haters. It's in their blood. They can't get rid of it. There are no Jews [in contemporary Poland], *they still hate them. It's acquired from generation to generation. Taught in the home. Taught in the churches. Everywhere. There were parts in Lwow we couldn't even go. There was a park, Stryjski, where they recognized somebody Jewish, they beat them up. In the university, they killed a Jewish guy when he insisted to attend the school; he was admitted to the school. But the Polish students, the anti-Semites, they killed him. We were getting uneasy and I wanted so badly my parents to go to Israel. So badly. The only lucky thing was the* [federal] *government wasn't very anti-Semitic. I mean there were anti-Semitic members but before the war Pilsudski* [statesman and de facto leader from 1926-35] *wasn't an anti-Semite.*

My mother believed that there was some attempt by federal government officials to halt the anti-Semitism that pervaded Poland. However, the rabid anti-Semitism that permeated the country was hard to stop.

Well, they were trying officially, the government was okay, but the people were anti-Semitic. There were high government officials who were anti-Semitic themselves. Look, the Jews tried to stay away from them. And they [Jews] *went their own way.*

A few years before the war, probably earlier than 1937, already, things were getting worse. There were like, pogroms. Students called themselves Enbecs. (I believe my mother is referring to the Endecja, a right-wing, anti-Semitic political movement). *I don't remember what the meaning was. They were all anti-Semite, anti-Jewish. They had demonstrations against the Jews. There was in the Parliament, a woman who couldn't stand it that the Jews had their Kosher ways, the Kosher killings of the animals.*

The Russians

Once the war broke out, life for the Jews went from bad to worse. At the start of the war, the Russians and Germans were allies. They divided Poland with the Russians occupying Poland east of the River Bug and the Germans west of the river. The Russians entered Lwow in 1939.

Well, the war broke out in 1939. I remember they were bombing Lwow. It was awful. It was so terrible. We were so scared. We were in the shelters. And the whole thing, I think, took seven days. And when we came out of the shelters, one day we woke up and the Russians were there. We didn't know what happened but then, that's what we heard, they made a pact with Germany. They took over part of Poland where it reached the river Bug. And the other part the Germans took over. West from Bug. And east of Bug the Russians took over. Though we were lucky enough that they [Russians] took over our [part].

The Russians were in Poland at the time I finished high school. With the Russians it was easy to get to college. So if the Russians stayed I could have. I was actually gonna go for medicine. In fact, when the Russians came to Lwow, nobody was allowed to call a Jew "Zhid." Nobody. They had to call them "Yivrey." In other words, Yivrey means, probably in translation, Hebrew. You could go to jail if you called somebody "Zhid." The government was not anti-Semitic, the Russian government.

The Germans broke their pact with Stalin and, in 1941, marched into Lwow turning the lives of the Jews upside down. By this time, the Jews had heard of what awaited them with the Nazis. The movement of Jews among European countries was not uncommon in the years before the war. For instance, my grandparents moved to Hungary where their oldest daughter was born and later returned to Poland. Just as my grandparents moved to Hungary, there were Jews who moved to Germany prior to the rise of the Nazis party. Once the Nazis came to power, the new dictate forced any Jew living in Germany, but born in Poland, to return to Poland. With little notice, they were repatriated.

Yes, we knew what they're doing. So, there was the Kristalnight where they were beating up, like a pogrom. They were smashing the windows in Jewish stores in Vienna. But nobody expected, even if a war would start, nobody expected that Poland is gonna collapse so fast. All Europe is gonna collapse!

Well, we didn't realize, we didn't know the war was gonna broke out. They were negotiating. See they were negotiating with England, Chamberlain. See this is what happened. They kept giving to Germany parts of Poland, Czechoslovakia. Germany, Hitler was never satisfied. First, he wanted the part of Czechoslovakia then he wanted a part of Poland, then he decided he wanted the northern part where the Baltic is. So they were giving in; they were appeasing him so there shouldn't be a war. So, nobody expected there would be a war. And everybody thought there's gonna be peace. Okay, he's gonna take this part of Poland and he's gonna take this part of Czechoslovakia and he's gonna sit quietly. Nobody expected what happened. Nobody in their wildest wildest imagination, nobody expected that this was gonna happen. We knew that they were throwing out the people from Germany. There were many people who in lived in Germany who originally were born in Poland and immigrated to Germany. And the Germans, when Hitler came, they started sending those people to Poland. And I remember we used to have them in our house. Some slept in our house. He just threw them out. He didn't let them take too much.

Well, we knew the Germans were persecuting the Jews. They were sending them out. They were killing them. They were shooting them. They were taking them out to public places and shooting them. People were running away from Poland the parts that the Germans took over. People were running away to our parts when the Russians were with us. They were telling us that they [Germans] were putting them into ghettos. They're shooting them. There's no food. There's all the horror. And in '41, they already had the concentration camps. Especially men, men used to run away. There weren't that many women. I think that in the beginning they just used to take the men to work, forced labor. They used to take men to forced labor. They used to put them in camps. Mostly men.

They [Poland] had to absorb them. I don't know if they were citizens, but I can't imagine they were not citizens, the Germans. I suppose they were Polish citizens.

Polish Jews felt increasingly threatened by the growing strength of the Nazis. Some Jews fled before the Nazis arrived. Others did not have the money or means to flee. Those who may have had the money could not liquidate their assets quickly enough to flee. Moreover, for most Jews of Europe there was nowhere to flee to. The Jews of every European country were threatened by the Germans and many by their own Christian citizens; the United States had a quota; the British closed Palestine to European Jewry. There were families whose older children left their families and fled. My mother's family stayed together.

Everybody was threatened, but you had no choice. Look, you live in a place. You have a family. You had an income. You can't just pick up and go. I wanted to go to Israel. I begged my parents. I wanted to go to Israel. I remember I was a teenager. I don't remember exactly what year. But not long before the war. It was about '36, '37 probably. I felt this is a place where the Jews should be. Actually, it wasn't Israel. It was Palestine then. I just had a feeling. I had a girlfriend who immigrated to Israel. She sent me a picture. I was so jealous that she's there and it's so beautiful in the picture. And you know, young children, young kids, teenagers, they have their dreams. Everything looks beautiful.

My parents were, you know they were considering it. But I don't remember how much money you had to have in order to bring a family to Israel. Because it was under the British mandate. The British put a certain amount of money you needed in order to immigrate. They didn't let everybody in. It was $10,000, I think. My father tried. He was figuring and figuring and finally I don't think they could come up with the money. Look in Poland to have dollars, you needed dollars to immigrate. It was dollars the British wanted. Maybe pounds, I don't know.

We never even thought about separating. Look, my sister had a boyfriend. She was getting married. Auntie Yanka had a boyfriend and she would have gotten married too. I was still in school. And my brother was still in school. And look, you don't think about those things. Here it's a little different. You go away to college. Over there you didn't even go away to college. You could count on your fingers the [Jewish] college students in Poland.

For the short period that the Russians occupied Lwow, Jews from Germany were allowed entry. However, there came a time when the Russians began to deport the Jews to Russia. My mother's family was not deported but only because my grandfather bribed the agents. Had my mother's family known that being in Russia would have saved their lives, they would have gone there.

After a while they were taking them away to Russia, deporting them to Russia. They were afraid that they were spies. Just like they were taking the rich people, they were considered "bourgeoisie." They were gonna deport us to Russia. They deported a lot of people, a lot of Jews to Russia. To all parts of Russia, even to Asia. There were many people who died on the trains going to Russia. They were doing it to Poles and Jews. If it wouldn't be for the Germans, they were much worse, the Russians were the epitome of everything bad. The Russians used to come in the middle of the night and take them *away. Take them from homes, put them on the trains. They were sending them to Russia, deep into Russia, to Asia, Siberia. It was scary. There were some people who wanted to go back to their families. They left their families on the western part of Poland where the Germans were. So they got them together and they told them they can go back to their families. They got them together, put them on the trains and sent them all* [to Russia]*; they said they're spies. You know in Russia everybody was a spy. You walked in the street, you talked to somebody, you looked back whether somebody's listening. We were always scared to talk, to say anything. You never knew who is listening and who is gonna go and denounce you. When the Germans started approaching Lwow, a lot of young people ran away into Russia. They went with the army with the front. After the war, they came back. They let them out. All the Polish citizens they let out.*

We had a neighbor who was such a good neighbor. We were so close together, very close together. Apparently, my father probably didn't even hesitate to tell him some things he shouldn't have told him. Jewish neighbor. And we later found out that he was the one who turned my father in to the NKG. It was the secret service then. And they took my father in and they told him he evaded the taxes or something. That he was a bourgeois. And they jailed my father. So it took us big big money to get him out. He was in jail for maybe two weeks. It cost us a lot of money to bribe the judge, to bribe everybody. They wanted taxes from him. A huge amount of taxes, which my father didn't even have. So finally, we got him out of jail. They took all kinds of grafts. There was a Russian lawyer, through the same neighbor, and he made a lot of money on us. I'm telling you, what some people can do, unbelievable. I think he [the man who betrayed them] *died. I saw her* [the man's wife] *once when the Germans were in Lwow. I remember that I was going into a bus once, I think I had my armband, Jewish armband. I was working, I think, or going outside of the ghetto. And she was probably pretending not to be Jewish. And I saw her on the bus, and I think she was scared of me. You know she went away fast. I don't even remember the year my father was in jail. But it wasn't too long before the Germans came in because they didn't send us out. We were always scared that they were gonna come and take us out, to Russia. Nobody knew where they're gonna send you* [in Russia]. *They put you on a wagon.*

We didn't expect that Germany is gonna declare war on Russia. Because basically they were fighting, they took over Europe, whatever part they wanted. The Russians, in the beginning, were retreating, and how! Listen, they [the Germans] *were in Stalingrad. They were near Moscow! They were deep into Russia and the Russians let them stay there in the winter and freeze to death. They let them stay in Stalingrad. They were in the city. They surrounded them. And they let them stay in winter. See, Russians are used to winter. They are prepared for it. The Germans were not prepared for winters like this. The same thing happened to Napoleon. They surrounded them. They cut off their supplies. Thousands upon thousands of Germans died there.*

Life Becomes Intolerable

When the Germans entered Lwow on June 22, 1941, life became intolerable for the Jews. They were forced out of their homes and herded into the poorest section of the city, where they were walled off. This became the Lwow ghetto. The Jews were allowed to leave the ghetto to work for the German war machine for specific hours of the day. They wore the Jewish star armband to identify them and had to be back in the ghetto when the curfew began. Once the Russians left Lwow, the Jews were faced with three enemies—the Nazis, the Catholic Poles and the Ukrainians. Interestingly, unless a Jew was dressed in religious garb, the Germans were unable to identify which Poles were Catholic and which were Jewish. The Poles and Ukrainians eagerly helped the Nazis by pointed out the Jewish citizens for them.

It came suddenly. The Russians had a pact with the Germans then they broke it. All of a sudden, the Russians started moving out, the Germans moved in. The Germans entered Lwow in June 1941. Oh, this was terrible. When the Russians withdrew, the Germans gave the Ukrainians and the Polaks free hand what they wanted to do with the Jews. They could go in and kill them and do anything they wanted. And they did. The Ukrainians and Polaks killed a lot of Jews before anything happened. Within a few months, all Jews were forced into the ghetto on the outskirts of town. There was fear. We were scared to death. People were fleeing to Russia with the army. The German army, they filled the streets. And the Polish people were all excited and happy. They were happy because they are anti-Semites and they hated the Russians.

The Polish people always hated Russians. Yeah, I think they rather have them [Germans] *than the Russians. Especially when the Germans started persecuting the Jews. For them, it was like a holiday. They were showing them every Jew. Every Jew, they showed the Germans. "Yudeh."* [Yudeh is the German word for Jew]. *In fact, I remember, in the beginning, we were walking down the street and a Polak came over to a German soldier and said, "Yudeh, Yudeh, Yudeh." And you know, the German soldier took us and brought us home. So, we can get home safely. It happened once in a while that you got to a soldier who was decent. So, he brought us home and he told us not to get out. This was unusual.*

Once in Lwow, the Germans began to tighten the noose around the Jews. The German campaign of public shaming, beatings and murder became daily events. The Jews were helpless to resist the Germans. At this point in the war, armed resistance or escape was impossible for most of the Jews of Poland.

There came a decree. Jews have to wear stars, the Jewish stars. Nothing was voluntary. You have to do it and this was the order! They were taking Jews. They were ripping their beards.

They took them in a public place and everybody [Poles] was rejoicing. And the Polaks were standing there and watching and they were beating them up. The men, only men, they used to take only men, especially if you had a beard, a religious man. They used to tear the beard and the peyas [side curls]. Beat them up. I saw one across the street from our window. I saw a guy with a beard. They were beating him up. I couldn't look. It was horrible, horrible. They were tearing his beard off and his peyas. They were full of blood. He was alone. Across from the window of our apartment, in an abandoned courtyard, I observed an innocent young man beaten to death. This had a profound impact on me and has never left my memory. The Germans used to gather people in the town square where they segregated them into groups. The young people were sent to labor camps. The children and elderly were sent to death. Many were shot at random on the spot. I still see those helpless children torn away from their mothers. I can't tell you the details. I don't want to try to tell you the details.

We stayed mostly indoors. We tried not to get out. You saw all the time, they were dragging people. I don't know where from. All the time they were dragging people, Jewish people. It's hard for me to remember all the details. I observed later, in the ghetto, when they came to take people. How they were loading them on the trucks.

Jews didn't have any arms. How could they be resistant? The Germans took France within four weeks, I think. Poland within three weeks. With all their arms, planes, soldiers, tanks and you know, like they were fighting a war. So how could the Jews? The Jews didn't have anything to fight with. They were unarmed. There was a force against them! A whole force! And besides this, besides the German force, there were Polaks who were helping the Germans any way they could. They used to recognize every Jew, go to the houses and get them out, chase them out. They were very helpful to the Germans. Very. There was always fear. The moment the Germans came in, there was fear all the time.

My mother and her family were forced to leave their homes and move to the most impoverished area of Lwow where the Germans had decided the ghetto would be. The Jews were given little notice that they had to leave their homes. The Jews of Lwow were on their own to find a place to live in the area designated for them. Jewish families took whatever they could get. These living arrangements turned out to be temporary. As the German's extermination of the Jewish population continued, the Lwow Jewish population declined. Once the walls of the ghetto were erected, thereby physically isolating the Jews from the Catholics of Lwow, my mother and her family had to move within the ghetto walls. The living area for the walled-in ghetto was now considerably smaller, forcing the Jews to live with one or more families in one apartment. My mother and her family shared an apartment with her Aunt Esther and her children, Zosha and Milek.

1941. It was in the winter. I don't remember the date. It must have been sometime in December. By the time they got around to putting us in the ghettos it was already winter. And I remember it was freezing, freezing cold when we were walking to the ghetto. They told us we have to go to the ghetto. They rounded up all Jews and marched us. Here you would say it was the suburbs. But it wasn't like fashionable suburbs. Suburbs in big cities in Poland were the lowest part as far as conditions. The Polaks, the Ukrainians had to move out and they placed the Jews there. This part of town consisted of homes and apartments with very poor and primitive facilities. And you know, there was no running water, the bathroom was outside, we had to haul the water from the pump to the house. It wasn't a "ghetto" until they closed it in. I know that there was a bridge into the ghetto that we had to pass. This they made the border of the ghetto. And then they surrounded it with a wall. They built walls! Maybe it was electrified. We had to go out and find our own apartment or houses or whatever was there available. We changed our apartment with a chimney sweeper, the guy who lived there. So we gave him our apartment with everything, with the furniture and we went to his apartment. Actually, I think it was a small house. We moved to another part of the ghetto once when they made the ghetto smaller. The part where we lived wasn't included so we had to move away from there. We had to move to the part that was still a part of the ghetto. I don't remember if we moved from the apartment to the house or the house to the apartment. Because, in the apartment we lived with our aunt who died [Mom is referring to her Aunt Esther who died years later in the U.S.], *you know Milek's mother. We lived with them together in one apartment. A two- or three-bedroom apartment. It was a pretty nice apartment, one of the new buildings. In fact, we had a bathroom and a bathtub in the house. It was my aunt, Milek, his* (Milek's) *sister, his sister's husband and then our family. It was my mother and father, we were three girls and a brother. We all lived together. I suppose you get used to everything after awhile. And we had to make the best of it.*

Young and able-bodied Jews were issued work cards that enabled them to work outside of the ghetto.

I was working in a German workshop where they were fixing German uniforms, soldiers' uniforms. There were a lot of Jewish girls. There were only women. Sewing. We were always anxious to work. We always hoped that people who are working they're gonna save. They'll need us. We used to go out to town to work so there was a certain time they used to bring us back. We used to go like in a column.

Among the worst horrors for the Jews of the ghetto were the sadistically evil aktions. Those people removed during an aktion were marked for death or sent to concentration camps. During an aktion, the Nazis shut down the ghetto for days or weeks at a time and the Jews were not allowed to leave their homes. Those who had work cards were safer than those without them because the Germans were less likely to kill them on the spot or remove them from the ghetto. During one aktion, my mother and her family hid in a dugout, a hole. They hid in it by placing wooden planks over the hole and then placing a bed over the planks. They hid in the bathroom covered with a wardrobe during another aktion.

All of a sudden, they came. You know people used to talk among themselves that tomorrow or the week after there's gonna be an aktion. They found out probably from someone from the Jewish authorities maybe. Or maybe someone knew a German who was friendlier. The Germans used to come with trucks and load up the people. They took 'em out, MARCH, MARCH, MARCH! They come to the apartment MARCH, MARCH MARCH, MARCH! They went to every apartment! They used to go to every apartment. And take people out and put 'em on the trucks. And nobody knew where they're taking them. Some of the people they took to camps, concentration camps, not to the gas chambers. Children, right away they disposed of. They shot them. Right on the spot. They killed them right on the spot. They threw them against the wall. I remember once how they pulled a child away from a mother. The mother was screaming. She was screaming, yelling. They just pulled away the child (Mom shakes her head). *A young child, maybe two or three years old. You know it's really hard to remember the details. There were so many, so many. They used to come and people were screaming, yelling. They used to tear them apart, families. It was just a horror. A horror. Putting people in trucks. Never knowing whether they'll come back. And I guess it turned out that many of them didn't come back. Later, we found out. I had a card that I was working. And I remember that everybody was hidden. We had a bathroom and we put a closet* [large armoire] *against the bathroom door. And I remember my aunt and the whole family was hidden there because they didn't have papers. They didn't work. First of all, they didn't take people this age to work anymore. My mother and father didn't work. So we showed them the card and they left us alone. Besides this, you had to be lucky too. I'm sure there were some people they took with the cards. I remember that once, a German came in, it was the aktion, and they came into the apartment, and everybody was hidden behind. I started washing the floor. The German came in and he looked that I'm washing the floor and he asked whether there's anybody and I said there's nobody here. So he didn't come in. Because the floor was wet. I don't know. It's luck. I remember once we were hidden under the floor. There was a hole dug out, like a cellar. You know, in Poland they didn't have basements. In the houses they dug out like a part of the floor because, even in the normal times before the war, when you wanted to preserve something, you know you didn't have a refrigerator or anything. And it was cold underground. So, you used to store things. And then on top they put planks like the floor to cover it. They used to put a handle and they used to pick up this top. We put a bed over it so nobody knew it was there. This is how we survived this aktion. We were all hidden. I remember this aktion lasted so long, a week or two. They were shooting! They were beating up! It was a horror! You just can't imagine! It's something you can't imagine. I remember not sleeping, not eating. I was so scared I had like a stone in my stomach. In the house there was food, but I couldn't eat. Ach!*

Mom shakes her head, distraught by the memory.

Nobody can imagine the fear, the intense fear and the horror that people went through when the aktion started. You can't describe it. Nobody can imagine it! Terrible. Even now, when I think about it, I just can't believe it that I lived through this. I remember when it was quieted down, someone used to get out and get something for us. But I couldn't eat anyway. I don't remember how long it was, but I remember a long time. I couldn't eat even if I had the food. They were just rounding up. They couldn't do it in one day, so they were rounding up.

In all the panic and fear, the Jews did not fight back.

First of all, they couldn't because they had nothing to fight them with. Second of all, everybody hoped that he's not gonna be the one, that he's gonna survive. You know, it became a survival. It was a survival. Individual survival.

My mother tells me about what happened to a cousin of hers in an aktion. This aktion spurred my mother and her family to seek places to hide outside of the ghetto walls.

Well, this was not long probably before the ghetto was liquidated. I was still in the ghetto. I remember it was an aktion when the Germans were running around all over and we were hidden under the floor. Nobody could really see that this was a hiding place. I remember hearing shots and I knew my cousin was outside. For some reason she didn't hide, or she just went out for some reason. And I heard shots and afterwards when everything was finished, I went out and she was dead. I saw her and she was dead. It was horrible. It was a horrible thing. There were people lying around dead all over. They just shot whoever they wanted. I couldn't hear exactly what the people were saying and why they were shooting them. But I know they were rounding up people and some of them they were shooting. I don't know what the reason was. They [Jewish police] took away the bodies. The Germans ordered the Jewish police to get people to bury the bodies. The Germans didn't do it, believe me. They didn't bury them. They made Jews do it.

My cousin [who was shot] only had a father. Her mother died when she was young. Tsila. She must have been in the late 20s. She was single. She didn't have family. She used to work in Lwow before the war. She was a waitress, I think. Her father was my grandmother's brother or cousin. He had like a little beer garden in the village. People used to come and, you know, buy beer. She decided she didn't wanna stay anymore in the village and came to Lwow and she was working. She was living with us at this time. I don't remember the reason she didn't hide. Maybe she had a job at this time and she didn't think they're gonna take her.

There did not have to be an aktion for the Germans to enter a home, office, workshop or factory and look for Jews to kill or round up to be shipped to extermination camps.

I started working in this workshop, and they started taking young people away. I don't know how they picked them. Some of them they took. Some of them they left. But we found out later that all those people went to Belzec. It was a small town not far from the Russian border. They used to kill them there. We heard that they're taking them there to dispose of them. Young, old, everybody. After a while, we knew what's going on. That's why I left the ghetto. I knew in the long run, I'm not gonna survive. Nobody's gonna survive the ghetto.

The overcrowding of the Jews in the ghetto combined with severe hunger made daily life wretched. Food rations allocated to the Jews were estimated to equal only one-fifth of the German and one-half of the Ukrainian or Polish rations.

They were rationing out food. My father had some money. If you had some money you organize some [food]. They used to give you coupons or something and you used to get the food there. The physical depravations were not those that brought our morale to its lowest point. They were the persistent persecutions, the systematic exterminations achieved through methods never known before in history and the hunger and dehumanization which permeated our wretched existence. We never had fights or anything about this. After a while the problem was survival. How to survive? And this was why we bought the papers that we eventually survived with. Papers from somebody from another town, I don't even know who it was. And, they were selling them. They were wheeling dealing. Through the gates there were the Polish guards. They were making a profit, the Polaks.

My mother's brother and other male family members were forced to work in a nearby concentration camp. Through bribes, they were able to free their male family members.

My brother worked too. He used to get out of the ghetto and he used to work until they took him to the camp. There was a, they didn't call it a concentration camp, but it was like a concentration camp. It was called Janowska. It was the part of suburbs. The street was Janowska and it was on the street, so they called it Janowska. They rounded him up. I know he was working for a watchmaker in town. He was coming out of the ghetto and going to work and coming back. And somehow, one day, they took him just like they took many people. It was a labor camp. They took people there to work. I remember we were coming out of the ghetto, my sister and I, and bringing food to them. They were working on the Jewish cemetery. Destroying the cemetery. They took those Jews from the labor camp to destroy the Jewish cemetery. So, I remember, we knew that they are there. And there was my cousin and uncle who didn't survive

90

and somebody else was there, another cousin or someone. And so we were bringing food to them because what they fed them they couldn't survive. We used to come out of the ghetto and kind of, you know, we were young girls. So, the guards, they used to look at us. They used to like it. We used to flirt with them [Polish and Ukrainian guards]. *So we used to come there to the cemetery and we were talking to them, in the meantime…*[food was sneaked into the male family members]. *You know, they took bribes too in this. There were people who organized those things and we finally got him out. We got out my brother and we got this cousin. This is how he survived. Otherwise he wouldn't have survived. And I think that my uncle got sick and they took him to the hospital and they finished him off there. But I think we had someone else there. Oh, my other cousin who used to live with us, he was there too and we took him out. So, we brought him back to our apartment, to the ghetto. This is how my sister* [Yanka] *got typhoid fever. Because they had lice. There was typhoid in the camp. And they came from there. Their clothes must have had lice, infected lice. She almost died.*

Sabotaging the work they did for the Germans was out of the question for the Jews because the repercussions were enormous.

Nobody sabotaged. See if one person sabotaged, they killed everybody. For each German soldier harmed, they would have killed out the whole neighborhood. They would have rounded out the whole street and shot everybody. And after all, look, people didn't know when the war's gonna end. People didn't expect that it's gonna last this long. And they thought, God, maybe maybe maybe it's gonna end soon and we're gonna survive. It's very very hard, you know, to explain to anybody who wasn't there, who didn't see it.

The Germans were masters at lying. They employed lies in order to prevent disorder and chaos. They were concerned that if they told the Jews that they were being transported to their deaths, the Jews might have done something to defy the orders or cause the Germans trouble. One tactic of deceit was to force the Jews, whom they were transporting to their deaths, to write letters to family members stating that they were fine. The Germans mailed the letters and killed their authors.

But what people don't realize is, is that it was so systematic and it was done so shyly. Because maybe they [Nazis] *were afraid that people shouldn't rebel or something. It's possible that they didn't want this to get out beyond Poland or Germany or whatever. Maybe they didn't want their own people many times to know. I really don't know the reason why they did it but they did it. They didn't want commotion. They wanted to do it quietly. They told you that you going to a labor camp and they took you to the gas chambers. They made them write, the people who were going to those camps, from the way, they made them write letters that they're going to labor camp and they're fine, and they're wonderful. Letters were coming and the people were dead by then. Later we found out. Listen, after all word got around after a while. After a while the Jewish police knew and the Polaks who were working there knew. Apparently, there were people who escaped by a miracle.*

The modus operandi of the Germans was to select Jews to administer the ghetto. In the Lwow Ghetto, the police and the administration were one and the same.

There were people who wanted a job. Their job was rounding up the people, keeping order in the ghetto. They [Germans] *told them they wanted a certain amount of people, so they went to homes and they took the amount they* [Germans] *wanted. So, if you knew a policeman, you could escape for a while. I don't know how long because the next time they came they got you anyway. I seldom saw even those policemen. They thought they're gonna be safe. Not for too long. They* [Jews] *didn't like them because they used to come and take people away just like the Germans. But, on the other hand, they couldn't help it. If they wouldn't, the Germans would have come to take the people anyway.*

My mother and her family decided that leaving the ghetto was a necessity if they wanted to survive. Thanks to their parents' remaining money and efforts, my mother and her sister, Lucia (Yanka), were able to get the birth certificates of deceased Catholic teenagers.

We all decided we had to do something. I said to my parents that I'm not gonna stay here because I knew that I'm doomed if I stay here. So, they bought me the papers. They arranged it. They bought the papers for me and my sister. I left first. I was the first one to leave. I didn't want to stay. I guess I was the most energetic. I guess I was the most scared for my life. When I came out, I didn't know what I'm gonna do. Originally, I thought I'm gonna be hiding throughout the war. Nobody knew how long the war is gonna be. I escaped in '43. I don't remember what month. It may have even been 1942 at the end. I was in Lwow with those gentile papers. I was working. My name was Anna Chaplinska. I had to memorize the birthdate. In fact, I was two years younger in the papers. I had to memorize, of course, the place where I lived. My other sister (my mother's oldest sister, Fanka) *had papers too but unfortunately, she didn't survive because they recognized her. She had a little crooked nose.*

When my mother decided she must leave the ghetto, she knew that doing so meant that she would need to hide outside of the ghetto, to somehow pass as a Christian, rarely see her family and ultimately turn her back on her Jewishness. Years later, when my mother began writing poetry, she wrote about her emotionally heart wrenching decision to move away from the ghetto.

Tear not my aching heart away
From all I have loved and lost, the day
I left to search for life elsewhere.
While Death would not allow to spare
A soul, but with a vengeance swept
The guiltless prey, while my eyes wept
A stranger to my own disguise
I fled the grip of cruel demise.

How do I live, survive in the wild
Away from a life with surroundings so mild?
How do I live when my heart bleeds and cries
In a world infested with deceptive lies?
With my mind overcast and my head reeling
No one to mend my dismal feeling,
The shadows, a ghostly remainder of past,
Would never depart from my exiled nest.
I saw wisdom fail and compassion die,
I saw deadly fear of vile betrayal cry
When the day of freedom from fetters arose
Only to die without purpose or cause.
From "Remembrances" by Anna Geslewitz

Fear remained my mother's constant companion. She feared her Polish Catholic neighbors. She feared the Nazis. She feared being caught. Every morning, her goal was to survive the day.

I was afraid. I was always afraid. All the time. It was a danger to go out in the street that somebody is gonna recognize you. You were always afraid, always scared no matter where you were.

Prior to the war, my mother's maternal cousin, Lonka, had married a Catholic man, Piotr, and converted to Catholicism. During the war, she lived in a cloister with him. Piotr saved her life and assisted her in helping her family members.

Lonka wasn't hidden. They were living in a cloister, with nuns. Lonka's husband found a job there. He was a handyman in the church there. He wasn't Jewish and she was converted before the war. She lived in Jaroslav, so nobody knew her. They had a little room and this is where they lived and he was working there. They already had a little girl. And they had some friends, so we paid those friends and they were hiding me. Eventually, my parents came out of

93

the ghetto and were hiding with another family. There were people who were arranging [hiding places for Jews]. *You paid them and they arranged for you those things. We kept in contact through Lonka.*

A Polish or Ukrainian woman was paid by my grandparents to set my mother up in an apartment. Having Christian papers allowed my mother more movement. Unfortunately for the Jews, those Poles or Ukranians who were paid by Jews to help them had the opportunity to question the motives of the person searching for work or a place to live. In other words, the suspicion was strong that the person was Jewish. With their heightened sense of mistrust of their Catholic neighbors, Jews were constantly worried about being betrayed. Betrayal meant that the Germans would be informed that the Jew was trying to pass as a Christian. The Christian Poles did not necessarily report their suspicions immediately. First, they bribed the Jews for money or valuables. Once a Jew had nothing more to give, the Christian would often squeal on him or her.

The woman who set my mother up in the first apartment became fearful of being suspected of harboring a Jew. My mother suspected that the woman who lived in the apartment may have squealed on her to other Poles since an acquaintance of the woman proceeded to blackmail my mother at her place of work. So my mother fled.

First, I was hiding out. I took off my band [armband with the Jewish star] *and I went to Lonka's friend's house and I was hiding out there. We were paying her. She did it for money. She didn't do it out of the goodness of her heart. That she's gonna take me in and my parents we were paying her. After a while, she decided that she didn't want to take a chance anymore. Now that I think about it I don't know if she helped me or she told the Ukrainians where I am. The woman who brought me there, I just had a sneaky suspicion. I don't know whether I'm right or wrong that she was the one that later* [sent people to blackmail my mother]. *They used to come where I worked, the Ukrainan boys, they used to come and they used to blackmail me. And I have a feeling it must have been from her family because they knew where I worked and she's the only one who knew where I'm working. Because for some reason they recognized me. So, when I had a watch on my hand, I gave them the watch and got rid of them. I had a watch. I had a ring. I had a necklace. Whatever I had. I didn't care. So I gave it to them and they left me alone for a little while.*

My mother then moved into a succession of different apartments. She had no choice since the people from whom she rented become fearful that they would be discovered harboring a Jew. The consequence for hiding a Jew was death or shipment to a concentration camp.

So I remember that we had another connection with some Ukrainian people and I was hiding out in an apartment with a single guy. He had a girlfriend. They were gonna get married. He would go away. I would stay in the apartment. I was hiding alone there. And I remember, I ate every day the same thing even so I was hungry. I got so tired of eating some kind of cereal. I used to cook it every day. Eventually he didn't want it either. He was afraid too. It was Lonka who took me out to find an apartment through a girl who came from a small town, a Polish girl and who had a room. She lived alone in the room. I guess she wanted a roommate to pay for half of the rent.

While passing as a Christian in her hometown, my mother worked in a building housing German soldiers and later in a book distribution facility. Since the Germans could not distinguish between a Jewish or Christian Pole, my mother did not worry that the Germans would become suspicious of her identity.

Now, before I went to Germany I was working in those places, for the Germans. I found a job in a German building and the soldiers were living in this building. I got a job in the kitchen peeling potatoes. You know who brought me there? One of those people, I think it was his sister, the guy who was hiding me, the single guy. I think it was his sister who brought me the first time to work there. But going back, I was peeling potatoes in the kitchen and a girl came in and she looked at me and she said, "Well, I don't think you belong here. This is not a job for you." And she gave me a better job, this was considered a better job, in the laundry room. She thought I was too sophisticated to sit in the kitchen and peel potatoes. And then I advanced to a maid. And I was cleaning the office in the officer's quarters. So, I had only one apartment I was cleaning. He had a radio there and everything and I was listening to music. It was a great job. I cleaned his room every day. I was straightening up, doing whatever I wanted. Nobody paid attention. What did they care?

While working in the building that housed the German soldiers, she was living in the first apartment outside of the ghetto with the woman she suspected told others who came to blackmail her.

This is the place where they used to come and blackmail me those boys. And I decided it's too dangerous. I didn't have anything anymore to give them. And if I don't have anything to give them, they'll, you know, they won't hesitate to turn me in. So, I had to find another apartment too because the girl [who was living alone] went back [to her home town] and she gave up the room.

So, I found a room with an old lady. It was a very nice section and a very nice apartment. And a nice room too. She lived alone the old lady. She had a son who lived downstairs. He was a drug addict. So, I guess she needed money for him. I think he was on opium or morphine, one of those. My sister was out of the ghetto too. I think she was working in a place where they were distributing books to the soldiers. It was a large distribution place. This is where I went to work after a while. I don't remember if I found the job or she found the job. She didn't have an apartment, so she came to live with me. So, we were together, in this lady's house, in one room in her apartment. We made our food ourselves. I just remember we were living there awhile and working and you know, we were pretty happy. We got information [about family members] *from Lonka. She kept in touch somehow. At this time my parents were hiding. They were out of the ghetto. Nobody in my family was in the ghetto anymore. See my parents were already hiding. Ukrainian people took them in, and they were paying them.*

One night, when my mother and aunt were in bed, there was a knock on the apartment door. They heard the landlady shuffle to the door and open it. Standing there were Nazis soldiers. They questioned the old woman about Jewish boarders. The landlady directed them to the building's superintendent. My mother and her sister decided they had to flee the apartment immediately. They soundlessly snuck out of the apartment into the dark night. They fled to the tiny crawl space where their parents were hiding. There, they all squeezed together for the night.

Listen. We were already in bed. We were already ready to go to sleep. Somebody knocks on the door. The landlady went to open the door and I hear them asking if living here are girls, the names and everything. Somebody squealed, somebody told them [the Germans] *that there two Jewish girls living in this apartment. So, they came after us. I knew it's no good. Who is gonna ask about us? Nobody knew us. They wanted some information from her. She didn't know so she told them to go to the superintendent downstairs to find out. We were so scared. Petrified. Absolutely petrified. We got dressed fast. I remember, all of a sudden, I got so hungry. I took whatever was there and I started eating. I never had this feeling. We got dressed fast. We left everything. We took off our shoes because we were on the second or third floor. We took off our shoes because we didn't want them to hear somebody's going down the steps. And we ran out of the house and we went to the place where my parents were hiding. We slept in this whatever you call it, this crawling space with my parents. I believe it was the spring of 1943.*

The Germans believed that the Poles were a lesser form of human but were judged to be good enough to work for them. Thus, the Germans allowed Polish Christian workers to come to Germany and work. To assist in the transfer of people, employment agencies were set up to pair workers with jobs in Germany. Those Poles who applied to work in Germany were civilian workers. Their wages, if they were paid, were lower and their ration of food was less than for a German. Some Catholic Poles worked without pay in exchange for food and lodging. The amount of food they received depended on where they were placed.

My mother and her sister decided that there was nowhere safe to hide in the city. They had to decide. They decided they had to save their lives by leaving Poland. The next morning, my mother and her sister went to an employment agency that sent Christian Poles to work in Germany. They would be safer in Germany as Catholics than in Poland as Jews.

The following morning, we went to the employment agency and volunteered to go to Germany. And when we came to this employment agency, there was a woman sitting a Russian woman, she was probably leftover from the Russians when they left. Somebody who would be more spiritual than I would believe that it was a miracle because I can bet 99% that she knew. That she recognized it [that my mother and sister were Jewish]. *We came there. We told her a story that we don't get along with our parents, that we don't we want to be with them. We told her the story. I don't know whether she bought it or not. She filled out the questionnaire and she asked us when we want the papers for. I said, "As soon as you can get it ready." She said, "Come in tomorrow morning." It was unbelievable that she would have it ready the following day. The following day we came. She gave us all the papers to go to Germany. Either she didn't suspect anything. But if she did, if she would have suspected, if she would have been real anti-Semitic, she would have said, "Uh, something is wrong here. Who are you?" I think that she knew. She recognized but she wanted to help us. That's the feeling I have. All we did in the morning, we went back to the apartment. We took the valises. We had two valises. We just took the stuff and left. You can't imagine. You can't imagine when you're scared like this, the way you think. There were a lot of miracles, that would be considered miracles to people who really believe in miracles. One night we slept in Lonka's place. We slept in her little room. Then the following day, we went to the train. We were going to Krakow. You don't even have time to think or anything. You go, you say goodbye and you leave. My father said, "Go and save your life," when we left. We didn't imagine that we're never gonna see them. But you know when the time comes, you have to run for your life, there's very little that you care about. You just look in front of you where you're going. You just escape. To get out. Just to get out.*

My mother's brother, Lonek, was supposed to be hidden. It seems that something happened within the family and he did not get to hide. Instead, my mother's aunt was going to the hiding place when she was caught. The aunt had a baby girl named Helen and a baby son.

They were supposed to hide Lonek in a cloister, a nunnery, in a church. They had a place reserved for him. But my aunt went. They caught her and they took her away.

She had a little girl and a little boy. So, the girl survived. She (Helen) *was hidden with a Polish family. The boy she put somewhere in front of a door, some Polish people and they recognized him, that he was Jewish, because he was circumcised. The Germans got rid of the baby. He was just a baby, a few months old.*

My mother did not find out what happened to her brother until many years later, when she read her sister's memoir. As it turned out, Lonek was the first member of her immediate family to be murdered by the Germans.

I didn't know where he was when I left. I don't remember if he was alive then. My parents, I think, didn't know where he was. But according to my sister, you know my sister left like a memoir. According to her, my brother was working for a watchmaker outside the ghetto. He was about 17, not even 17. And one day the Germans came and took him out of the store and shot him right there. And according to her, I don't know, I didn't see it but according to her somebody who saw told her. My parents didn't even know. They always hoped that maybe they took him to someplace, maybe a labor camp and he's gonna survive. I don't remember what we told my parents, but it would have been a horrible thing if they found out.

At the time when I got out, the ghetto was still there. Everybody was still in the ghetto. But, after a while, everybody got out. My parents got out of the ghetto too. He [the person who was hiding them] *was Ukrainian. They* (my parents) *were paying. They were paying their way. They were constantly paying them. They were hiding underneath the floor. There was a little basement. Only my parents. This is where they were until, I later found out when I was in Germany already, that they gave them out. Maybe they didn't have any more money left.*

My mother lost track of her oldest sister. She later learned from Lonka that Fanka had tried to flee to Germany, was caught and murdered.

I don't know where Fanka was. She was trying, Lonka later told me. She came out of the ghetto. She also had papers. I didn't know what happened to her but Lonka told me after the war that she went also to the employment agency. She wanted to do the same thing (flee into Germany as my mother had) *but someone recognized her. A Polak recognized her. They killed her. See those people they didn't take them to the camp, who they caught. Because they considered they were cheating on them; they wanted to get away. See, my oldest sister was supposed to get married. Before the war, she had a boyfriend. And when the Germans came and took him away, she really didn't care to live anymore. They took him away. I don't know what happened to him, but they killed him. They didn't fool around.*

Everyday life for the Jews was defined by constant fear and suspicion of the Catholic Poles. Within the confines of this horrendous everyday existence was the drive to save oneself. If a family member, such as my mother's sister Fanka, "looked Jewish," her "Jewish appearance" put anyone she was with outside of the ghetto walls in danger. Thus, my mother and Yanka had to make the horrific decision not to house Fanka with them outside of the ghetto. This is what the Nazis and Polish citizens inflicted on the Jews.

The times were so, you were afraid, you know, you saw her across the street, you afraid to talk to her. Nobody can imagine even what was going on! Somebody, a Polak is gonna recognize her so he's gonna recognize you! You were afraid! You were constantly looking if someone is following you.

Lonka's conversion to Catholicism, upon her marriage to Piotr, meant nothing to the Germans. Thus, her life was also in constant peril. The nuns in the cloister thought she was Catholic, so they did not bother her. However, asking them to give assistance to Jews was out of the question. The nuns in this cloister hid no one.

Lonka was hiding herself!! She wasn't hiding in a cellar. She was (hiding in the) open. She was his wife. She was Jewish but they didn't know. She didn't go anyplace. She was trying to survive where she was.

When I ask my mother why the nuns did not hide Jews, she angrily struck back at me.

"Why? Why don't you ask them?"

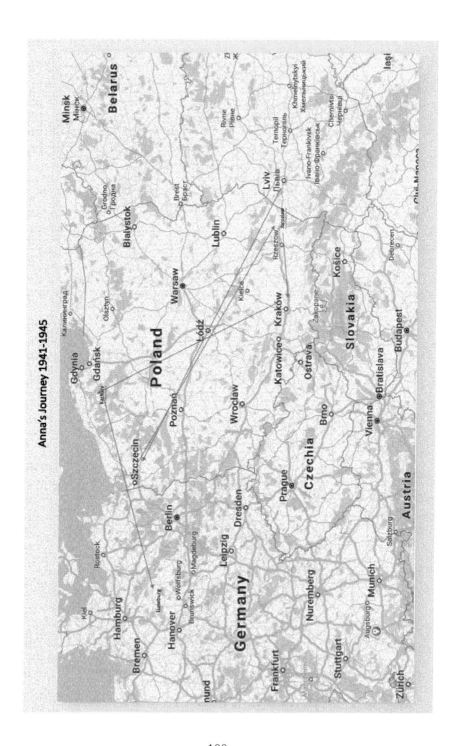

Anna's Journey 1941-1945

Escape

My mother and her sister took the treacherous trip out of Poland into Germany. There was never a moment when they could let down their guard. There were the Catholics who might suspect them of being Jewish and the Germans who inspected identity and travel documents to make sure that no Jew would escape their grasp.

You know, when we were going to Germany, we had all our papers. And we came to Krakow. And between Lwow and Krakow there were inspections. This was another miracle. We were sitting in the train and we were sitting next to a German soldier. We spoke German so we could converse with him. Oh, before this. They didn't leave you alone. They were watching the trains, the buses, everything! They were watching out for Jews. Those were German Gestapo probably. Or they worked for the Gestapo. They came to check the papers, people's papers. And they come to us and they ask us about our papers. I show them the papers. They start asking me questions. What's your name and this. In situations like this, I figured look, they're going to really question me I won't be able to answer all those questions. But I said, "Can't you read? You have my papers. You can read. See what's in it." And you know they left me alone. They gave me back the papers and they left me alone. And going back to the soldier who was sitting next to me. When we arrived in Krakow, we had those two valises. And he said, "You know what? Take those two valises and put them in the German compartment." There was a separate compartment where the soldiers and Germans, only Germans, had the valises. He came with us to this compartment, into this booth. He said to somebody who was servicing, "Take these two valises because we have to wait." We had to wait a few hours. About two hours, I think, in Krakow for the next train to Katowice. We put the valises there. So, we were sitting, there was a little garden in front of the railroad station. There were benches. And we're sitting there and talking and we see a guy walking around. Wherever we go, he goes. Wherever we sit, he sits. He just didn't leave us alone. He kept his eye on us all the time. All the time. I knew he's after something. Finally, I said to my sister, "Let's take a look if the train is there. Maybe the train is waiting there." We went there and we went to pick up our luggage in the German compartment. He saw us going to the German compartment and he left. He thought either we are German or we're something. Why would we have the luggage in there? So this is another miracle. And the train was waiting. The train was already on the station. We went into the train and as soon as we left the Polish soil, we were breathing with ease already. There were mostly Germans and they didn't recognize, wouldn't know [my mother and her sister as Jewish]. *In fact, when we had the valises on top and we had to change, they were helping us. The guys, the Germans, they were helping us to take the valises down. They were very courteous. I believe this was spring 1943. I'll tell you, when we were in Germany, on German soil, we just breathed with ease already.*

We got a place to work and we were actually supposed to go to the western part of Germany. But, the train stopped in a place, Lechnitz, and we met some Polish people. We told them we ran away from a transport going to Germany. And they said, "Tell them that you lost your group and they'll send you to a job here." They thought we were Polish. They said that there are trains going to Kiel and from Kiel going to Sweden. In fact, there were trains from there, it was northern Poland, the trains were going from there to Rostock, I think was the Baltic port. They were going to Sweden. They told us we could go there and hide out in those trains to Sweden. Everyone wanted to escape! I was afraid someone was gonna catch us. I decided I'm not gonna take a chance. I didn't know how safe it is. I didn't want to do it. See, if we would have been Polish maybe I would have done it. Because we were not, I was afraid once they're gonna catch us and they're gonna start asking questions, we were done. It was the worst thing. Once they start asking questions, you're finished.

My mother and her sister decided not to take the jobs in Germany that the woman at the employment agency in Lwow had found for them. Instead, they went to a local employment agency.

So we went to the employment agency near Szczecin. It was a German city. [It was named Stettin when occupied by the Germans]. *Now it's a Polish city. I went to the employment agency. I told them we got lost from a group and if they have a job we'll stay here. And they gave us a job. They gave my sister a job with a farmer. I was a maid and doing just housework. Her job was a little harder.*

My mother was placed in the home of a well-to-do German family. She was to be their maid. For her services as a maid, she was given room and board.

I had a room in the attic where I was sleeping. They cooked. They didn't even let me cook. He [head of household] *was married a second time. He was a pretty wealthy guy. He was dealing during the war with grain. He was a wheeler-dealer. He used to get meat and everything. There was everything in this house. We didn't eat at the same table with them. We ate in the kitchen with the other people who worked there. There were two other people, two men who worked there for them. Polaks. I was afraid more of them than of all the Germans around there. There were a lot of Polaks in this little town. We all used to get together. You should have heard the language they used* (Mom rolls her eyes and laughs). *I wasn't used to it, but eventually you get used to it and you start talking like they do.*

I remember when the planes used to come and throw bombs. We had a munitions factory not far from where I was. Peenemunde. They were constantly bombing so they were flying over us, over our town. They used to have the alarm. They used to go to the basement and hide. We were so happy. We just wanted to stay there and wave to them, that they're coming.

There was one incident I remember. He wanted me, my boss, to clean his shoes. I thought that I was too good to clean his shoes. I didn't wanna clean his shoes. He said, "You know Anna, you don't wanna clean the shoes? I'm gonna send you to Peenemunde." (Mom laughs). The munitions factory. The next day he had the shoes cleaned and in front of the door. (Mom laughs).

He was a fat guy. I think he was much older than his second wife. She was a nice woman. She worked in the office with him. That's why she was allowed to have a maid, two maids, because she worked. He was the boss. He did whatever he wanted to. Well, most German men, I don't know today, but in those days most German men were bosses. The wife didn't have much to say.

I felt safe. I was never afraid of the Germans because they would have never known [that Mom was Jewish]. I was only afraid of the Polaks.

She [Yanka] lived not far from me. I used to walk to her. She was doing all kinds of jobs because they were farmers. They had pigs. She had to feed the pigs and she had to do other chores that I didn't have to do. See the family I worked for mainly needed us as maids, to take care of the kids, to clean the house. I didn't even cook. The daughter used to cook.

My mother seemed to have a good relationship with the German family for whom she worked.

My boss she was the second wife of this guy. His first wife died. So, he had an older daughter who was about my age. And then he had three little kids with her, this second wife. The little one was Ooshi, older one was Marsa, and the oldest was, I forgot. Koch [last name]. I took care of the kids. I dusted. I cleaned. I remember I used to sew. I used to sew for the daughter and she used to clean for me. She used to do things for me [Mom laughs]. Otherwise I wouldn't have the time to make her clothes. She was a little dumb. She was a very pretty girl. Big, tall and husky. A wholesome looking girl. She used to tell me she had a boyfriend who was in the army, in the front. She used to tell me everything. Every time she got a letter, she used to tell me what he writes in it. One day, I told her I can predict from cards what's gonna happen. I didn't know a thing about it. I didn't even know the difference between the cards. Whatever she used to tell me I used to tell her later and she said, "Ya, ya, ya. That's true." She didn't remember she told me!

One day, mother got a letter from Lonka.

Irka was with Lonka. And she was really in danger. She was afraid too that someone is gonna recognize her. She [Irka] got papers too. Lonka asked me if I knew whether there's room for somebody else there too. So, I asked my lady. I said, "Look I have a cousin who would be willing to come too and work. Do you need somebody else?" She said, "Sure." Why not? For nothing they had people working for them. I remember I went to Szczecin. Now it belongs to Poland but before the war it was German. I went with her [boss]. We went by train. And we made out all the papers for Irka. In fact, when I went with her and we came back, she was telling, the daughter, the oldest daughter there, "De veist, Anna est eine lady." [You know, Anna is a lady]. *We went to a restaurant. She bought food to eat there.*

Lonka, having been in touch with family members, was the one who learned of their fates. She wrote my mother about her parents while my mother was working in Germany.

Lonka wrote us a letter when we were in Germany. She wrote in the letter that the parents are not alive anymore. Well, they were in touch with them, Piotr, her husband. Yeah. The people who were hiding them, they themselves called the police on them. Maybe they ran out of money. I don't know. So, they had no reason to hide them anymore. I found out when my parents, when they killed my parents. When we wrote letters to each other, we had to write not in a straight language. It was like when you write something and it has a different meaning. She wrote that our parents are gone. In 1943, I believe also they liquidated the ghetto and nobody stayed. They were so afraid that a Jew shouldn't stay that they burned the ghetto. Because they knew that some people are hiding. They had hiding places. They couldn't go every place to find a hiding place. So they burned the whole ghetto.

My mother's grandparents were in their seventies and eighties when the Germans arrived in their village.

They were killed. No doubt about it. They were killed. What did they do to old people like this? They were over 70. They were probably closer to 80. What do they need them?

Six months prior to her liberation, my mom and Irka were sent to dig trenches for the retreating German army.

The Russians were coming closer, about six months before we were liberated. Maybe not even six months. The Russians were coming from one side and the Americans from the other side closing in on them. They were losing the war. So, they sent us to dig trenches. The Germans. The authorities. They took away people from jobs that they didn't think were necessary. My sister they didn't take because she was with a farmer. The workers who worked for farmers they didn't take away.

As they dug trenches, the laborers were moved from place-to-place. They slept where they could. Food was rationed and scarce.

Uh, where we lived! We lived in schools. We slept on the floor, on the straw. Wherever. See we didn't stay in one place. They kept shipping us out. Wherever we dug, they shipped us further. One place we lived, I don't know what it was, a school or just a barn? In one place in a barn. [We slept] with other Polish women. They fed us so we could survive. They rationed out bread. I don't remember how much. They didn't feed enough. But I had an older guy who was watching us because everybody was in the army there. All younger people. This was an old guy close to 70. There were some Polish girls they were really husky husky girls. The guy said to me, "Anna, leave it to them. They can do it." He didn't make me do anything. It was just that we didn't have enough food there. So, we used to go to the local farmers there. There were Polish people working. Irka's incredible. She went to a Polish guy on the farm and she told him that I love him [Mom chuckles]. And the guy brought us food. But I had a lot of trouble because I didn't wanna bother with him. One of the guys who worked with me in Lechnitz, where I was a maid, he sent me some food. I remember he sent me a jar of jelly and some bread. So, we had a little bit more than other people. And then, one day I discovered that there was a Polish camp for the prisoners of war. We befriended some of those Polish guys. They didn't let them out but where we stayed it was almost across the street, the camp. They were behind the fence. We could communicate with them. We talked to them. They used to get from Red Cross the rations. They got chocolate and cigarettes and all kinds of good things. Cans. I remember they gave us once a whole package with food. I was with other people and I didn't like the idea either because when people have a little better everyone else is jealous. I was just afraid that somebody shouldn't say, you always had in back of your mind that you're Jewish. That somebody's gonna recognize you.

Actually, the last place I was working, at the trenches, I worked in the infirmary. In the hospital. We had it pretty good because I was the only one who knew how to write and read German. They had Russians, Italians. The girl there in the infirmary, the German nurse, she liked one of the Italian guys and she kept him in the infirmary, sick all the time [Mom laughs]. This was before liberation. I'm just telling you because it was so funny.

Look, but it was better than a concentration camp anytime. But I was always afraid of the Polaks they shouldn't recognize me. At this point, I wasn't so afraid. The papers I had were from, I think from Rzeszow. And it was already taken by the Russians so they they couldn't check it anymore. Suddenly we heard that the Russians are coming closer and closer. And one day they were there.

I was liberated in January 1945.

Liberation

Once liberated, my mother and her cousin needed to figure out where to go, how to get there and how to get there safely. They also needed to get food somehow. Even though they were liberated, my mother and her cousin were afraid to go back to their Jewish identities.

We were still Polish. We didn't admit that we were Jewish. I didn't want to take a chance. We were so scared that we didn't take a chance. This is when it started, another chapter because we didn't have a place to go. There was no food. There was nothing. When we were liberated, we don't know where we were going. We had no place to go! We could have gone with the Germans, but who wanted to go with the Germans? The war was going on! The Russians liberated us. And what was going on there with the Russians too [Mom shakes her head]. Uh! Don't ask! Uh, the girls there and they wanted the girls and you had to hide. You had to use all kinds of tricks to get away from them.

When the Russians came, when we were liberated, we didn't have anything to eat. Look it was such a, it was an incredible time. We had a valise with clothes. We couldn't even carry it. We were so weak we couldn't carry. I don't remember whether I left it someplace or carried it. Jane [Yanka] wasn't liberated yet because she was further west. She stayed with the farmer. I was just with Irka. Irka suggested we go to Jaroslav [where Lonka was]. But the transportation in those days were not like now. We were hitchhiking all our way. Hitchhiking and we had to wait for trains. You know, cattle trains. Once in a while you caught a passenger train. Whenever you caught a train, you went on it. Before you got to a big city, you had to hitchhike. You didn't even know where you're going sometimes. So, wherever we saw a truck, we used to hitchhike.

And food. There was no food and no way of getting the food. We were so hungry. We didn't know where to turn. I remember the train stopped in a village. There were farmers. We went to beg for food we were so hungry! And while we were coming back the train started and we were running like crazy and they pulled us up to a different wagon. You didn't know when the next train is gonna come! You had no place to stay! It was in the middle of winter. It was so freezing. We were so cold. I remember I had a blanket that I took with me. We were sitting, Irka and I, in a corner covered with this blanket over the head. It was freezing! It was absolutely impossible. I remember running through the meadows. The train started moving. Ugh, we ran and ran. I remember I almost got a heart attack. I fell and I couldn't move. Irka came and she said, "Let's go! Let's go!" The train was moving already. Some guys picked us up to the train.

Wherever Russians passed they left Polish police. They organized the Polaks to administer the cities and the towns. This way, somehow, we came to Bitgusczyk. This was the next city.

And there was already the Polish police. We wound up in one of the hotels. Everything was a chaos. Everything. We slept there in a hotel. It wasn't like it used be like a hotel. They supplied for the people who were running away from the Germans, coming back to Poland. They had to have a place for them to sleep. The Russians gave over to the Polaks the administration. Somehow, we got food. People were living there. We dragged on, dragged on until we came to Jaroslaw. We got back on a train, then another train until we got to Jaroslav. Lonka was already there and she had an apartment, so we stayed with her. And then, it was really for the first time that we had a little bit of our normal life.

But all those memories, I'll tell you, I don't know if people who went through are trying to erase many of those memories. Or, I don't know, it's for myself, it's hard to remember details. It's also hard to want to remember things. Because it was a horror. Just something that no one can imagine unless if you went through it.

In their wake, the Germans left utter chaos. Displaced people, fleeing German soldiers and concentration camp survivors converged into human mishmashes on the heaps of German-made rubble.

You should have seen this exodus of people from wherever they were liberated. Everybody! Polish people and I saw Jewish people coming from the concentration camps going back, on the train. I saw people that were liberated and they were like walking skeletons. They were just moving slowly, like ghosts. Their faces, their bodies, they were skin and bones. They had rags. It was a terrible sight. It was an awful sight. Now that I think about it, nobody can ever ever imagine what the people looked like. Like wandering skeletons! They were talking Hungarian. A lot of them were Hungarians. They were going back to Hungary. This is why they were on the trains going south because Hungary was south of Poland. I remember they had pots. They didn't even have the strength to go to the bathroom. So, they used those little pots. To me it seemed so disgusting. I wasn't used to it. I don't know whether they were eating from them. Nobody did anything. Nobody asked anything. Everybody was going their way. Everybody just wanted to get to the destination and start all over again. The first time that I really saw what was going on in the camps was on television when I came here to the United States.

My mom left for Germany penniless and returned to Poland penniless. She settled part-time in Jaroslav and began selling cigarettes on the black market. She also did a bit of traveling to find surviving relatives.

When we came to Poland, we were in Jaroslaw but we used to smuggle cigarettes from one part of Poland to another part and selling them. Everybody was doing it. I took a chance. I had to take a chance if you wanted to make a living. You got to live on something. I didn't have any money. I didn't have any clothing. I didn't have anything. So, I took a chance. Food was there if you had the money. You could go to a restaurant and eat only if you had the money. There were people who had jobs. They were paid on the jobs. But there was more money in black market. Everybody was on black market. We used to bring German marks from northern Poland and exchange them, bring them to Katowice.

I didn't live in with my cousin in Jaroslaw all the time. I lived a part of the time Krakow. My aunt [Esther] was there. You know, Milek's family. They were hidden somewhere, all of them. They paid them. But I don't know, maybe at the end they didn't have money; they saw that the war was ending and they kept them. They survived.

Once my mother and Irka were shipped out to dig trenches, they had no contact with Yanka.

The war ended; we didn't hear from her. I went to look for her. I went with Irka. I didn't know where she was. So, we decided to take a trip to northern Poland; we're gonna look for her. And we took a train and we went. We didn't know where we're going. But we thought we're gonna find some of the people who worked in the same village. It was a little town. And we found a guy who was working in the same (place). And he told us to go to another place and ask somebody else because supposedly they saw her go with this guy.

She didn't know where we are and we didn't know where she wound up. We took trains and trains. It was far. Very far. We had to go from the southeast of Poland northwest. It was a very tedious ride. The trains were not going on time yet. We used to sleep in the stations. One night we slept on a table in a railroad station. There were no hotels. There was no place to be then. We didn't know anybody. We finally tracked her down. We found one of the Polish people who worked with us [in Germany]. He told us that my sister is in Kartuzy which is a small town not far from Gdansk which is by the Baltic Sea. Gdansk used to be in German Danzig. It was a free city before the war. We found her there [in Kartuzy]. She was already working there for the city government, I believe. Did we surprise her! I hid and she came came into the building where she lived. Somebody told her to go where I was hiding. I came out and she couldn't believe it! She was so surprised! And I was crying, crying. She was the only one left in my family. I just didn't know if I'll ever find her. She wasn't looking for us. We were looking for her. I don't know why she never came to Jaroslaw or wrote a letter. And when we came there, we moved together with her. She had a room and she had a job. After a while I opened a store with sewing notions. We had clothes on consignment. And we had some fabrics. I went to larger cities to buy the notions for the store.

My mother, Yanka and Irka stayed in Kartuzy a few months and then left for Germany. For most Polish Jewish survivors, Poland was a country of hatred and now the world's largest Jewish cemetery. They had no interest in living there again.

The post war years were a whirlwind of confusion for the survivors, and they lived in a state of limbo. They desperately searched for family members. hoping to find someone who survived. Signs asking about family members were posted wherever Jewish communities sprang up. Survivors travelled where they hoped they might find a family member. Existence was day to day with nothing tying them to any particular location. The survivors were rootless, stateless and, in too many cases, the sole survivors of their families. Surviving Jews from all over Europe converged into different German cities hoping to use the cities as transit points to the United States, Canada or Israel. My mother just happened to land in Lüneburg because a cousin was there. That was in 1946. It was in Lüneburg that she met my father.

We found Auntie Yanka in '45. In 1946 in the spring we left. We didn't want to stay in Poland. There was no future for us in Poland. I didn't want to stay all my life Anna Cheplinska. Even after the war, I remember when I was in Krakow and they had the pogrom. The Polaks were running around with sticks and breaking windows. If they caught a Jew, they beat him up. We decided to go to Germany. There was a chance to go from Germany to the United States or Israel or someplace. So, we registered as Germans. We went to the authorities that were resettling those people. My name is actually German. Gersten is a German name. And we went with the German refugees to West Germany. I remember I buried all my Polish papers somewhere in Gdenya, I think. I was glad to get rid of them! I registered in my real name, Anna Gersten. Everybody in those days called me Hanka, Anna. I figured it's too difficult for me to start changing [back to Charlotte] *again. Anyway, we went as German refugees. Irka had her brother, Marion, in West Germany. So, we went to him. Lüneburg, Lüneburggehide. This was the only person we knew. It was already organized there. There was a Jewish community. And they had a place where they used to get together. They used to get people a place and then eventually you found a room with Germans. Most of the people were from concentration camps there.*

We abandoned the store. Nobody even realized that we were leaving. I had there a woman working for me in the store. Before we left, I told her to give back the clothes to all the people who gave the clothes on consignment. I had it all marked, the names and everything. It was all organized. Whatever belonged to us, I put in the valises. I had two or three valises full. Piotr and Lonka came and they picked up the valises. I gave them a lot. I don't know what they did with it.

Yanka had a boyfriend then, Richard. He was a Polak. He was a very intelligent man. He was a professor in Warsaw at the free university. He was married. In fact, he had a little boy. The boy came to visit once. An adorable little boy. The wife came too. He didn't want to stay with his wife. I don't know if he was divorced or he was getting a divorce. He came with us. He was there and Irka was with us. And there was Irka's cousin. Her name was Hanka. She had dark hair. We called her Charna [black] Hanka because the difference between me and her. [My mother began using Anna after she had been in U.S. a number of years.]

Marriage

Survivors met and married serendipitously, hoping to start life anew. The old order of matchmaking was gone. The new order was a hodgepodge of matches. In the old order, young people married others of similar economic and educational backgrounds. A privileged upbringing or level of education meant little in the new order. The new order was to restart one's life, as soon as possible, with a partner. Thus, it came to be that my mother, who was well educated and from a well-to-do home, married my father, who had an eighth-grade education and whose family was, economically, low-middle class.

My parents married on August 29, 1948. Prior to receiving a visa to Canada or the United States, my mother applied to enter medical school in Germany. She was accepted. I do not know the timeline for her acceptance but I know that she declined the offer. Instead, pregnant with me, she came to the United States, in January 1950.

My mother's paternal uncle Simcha and aunt Sara perished in the Holocaust. Simcha had two sons, and Sara had a boy and a girl. All perished. Uncle Hirsh and aunt Esther and her two children, Milek and Zosha, survived. My mother's maternal aunts Gittel, Mincia, Yetta and Hudka and her uncle Moshe died. One of the cousins, Helen (the daughter of Hudka and Izhio), was hidden by Polish Catholics during the war. After liberation, when her father came to get her, the Polish family refused to give her to him. Izhio had to get a court order to get his daughter back.

As she approached middle age, my mother took up writing poems. Most of the poems are related to the Holocaust and exude emotions that were either repressed or too difficult for her to talk about.

I have so many emotions. To me, I don't know if it's the reminder of what I went through, but it seems like we are never safe anyplace. We should always remember. You have to constantly watch and see that it shouldn't repeat. I don't know how. The situation's now different. First of all, in the United States it's a different situation because they have so many races and denominations. So many different people from so many countries coming, so many races. And I think that the American people, they have many groups here, many anti-Semitic groups, but I still think that the American people basically are much more tolerant than any other country in the world. The Polaks, they're only Polaks. There are very few religions or other races [in Poland]. In fact, there are no other races. Except for a few Jews that are left, maybe a few Germans. It's just a mixture of different people here. It's such a mixture that it's very hard to imagine that any one group could win here and oppress any other group. The people are different. The people have a different mentality here. I think so. So hopefully it's not gonna happen.

Though there's no assurance anyplace. Then, the other part I think is Israel. The existence of Israel is probably the most important, the single thing for the Jews. Even so, I don't think the American Jews, many of them don't realize it, how important Israel is to us. To our safety. Look, if we would have had Israel when it all happened, people would have gone to Israel. They would have left. But nobody wanted to let us in. Nobody, including the United States.

My poems are a reflection of my emotions and everlasting pain and distress that was a direct result of my experiences in the Holocaust. In the years after the war, those recurrent visions and memories intensified. The need to express them compelled me to write poems. All the people, places and events in the poems are real.

For many years after the war, I tried to delete the horror pictures from my memory. Instead, the memories intensified. My continuous inner pain and the inhumanity of the Germans, Poles, Ukrainian, Lithuanians and Austrians still linger in my memory like an indelible picture. The escape route I took, by assuming a Christian identity, still brings distressing emotions and recurrent visions. The nearly complete destruction of the European Jewish population and the horrifying way this goal was virtually attained, haunt me to this day. The distortion of the truth, the lies and blame placed on the Jews for all the world's ills, have left a permanent mark on my soul.

And though the sign upon my brow
Has paled in soothing sunshine glow,
My wounded heart cannot erase
The Memory's remaining trace.
from "The Clouds of Freedom" by Anna Geslewitz

114

What to Do With The Jews?

1945-1950

Liberation for the Jews did not come for all at the same time. The lucky ones were liberated early in 1945. Thus, as it happened, my mother was liberated by the Russians in January 1945, while in the German heartland the Germans continued to enslave my father until May 1945.

Europe, when the Germans surrendered, was a continent in utter chaos. The postwar bedlam began as the Russians and allies began liberating section upon section of Europe. The Russians marched westward while the Americans and British marched eastward, eventually meeting in Germany. I remember my mom telling me that the movement of people was unimaginable. Not only movement. Survivors were desperate to get news of loved ones. Millions of displaced people traveled any way they could trying to find a place to land. My mother traveled by foot, wagon, and in a cattle car train back to Poland. My father walked from the concentration camp to the nearest city. Polish laborers and German soldiers sat on public transportation with skeletal concentration camp survivors. Hungarians headed south while the Poles headed east. Defeated German soldiers tried to return home disguised as Jewish victims. The jumble of peoples was enormous and the migration of nationalities was massive. Historically, it was without precedent.

The American and British armies had their work cut out for them as they began liberating European Jewry. They had mounds of rotting corpses, skeletal humans who were sick, vermin infested, and barely alive and a German population indifferent to what they had done. The allied armies were confronted with a humanitarian disaster of unparalleled proportions. The infrastructure and funds necessary for the colossal humanitarian crisis came at the expense of the victors, primarily the Americans and British. The American Jewish community knew that sizeable amounts of monies would be needed to help European Jews once the Germans were defeated. They had begun amassing the funds soon after the war began. But the funds were severely inadequate to cope with the millions of displaced Jews and their massive needs.

Soon after Europe was set free from the Germans, American, British and French set up camps for the displaced (DP camps) in Germany, Austria and Italy. Each country had its own procedures for helping the Jews. In other words, there was no uniformity. Survivors were housed in military barracks, hospitals, hotels, private homes and various other locations. Millions of displaced individuals needed to be fed and treated for health issues resulting from years of filth, starvation, and physical and mental traumas.

Reparations and Restitution

In this new world, European Jewry had to survive and build their lives anew. Their survival was dependent on a number of factors, two of which were housing and food assistance. Jewish organizations, worldwide, came together to help the survivors by forming the umbrella Jewish Restitution Successor Organization (JRSO).

On March 31, 1946, the Jewish Restitution Successor Organization (JRSO) was designated as successor to heirless and unclaimed property belonging to European Jews. In the same year, the organization was incorporated under the New York State membership corporation law. The incorporators were: The American Jewish Committee, the American Jewish Conference, the American Jewish Joint Distribution Committee (JCD), the Board of Deputies of British Jews, the Commission on European Jewish Cultural Reconstruction, the Council for the Protection of the Rights and Interests of Jews from Germany, the Jewish Agency for Palestine, and the World Jewish Congress. Later the following organizations were included: Agudas Israel World Organization, the Anglo-Jewish Association, the Central British Fund, the Conseil Representative Israelite du France, and the Arbeitsgemeinschaft Sueddeutscher Landesverbaende Juedischer Gemeinden. In recognition of the special role of these bodies as the operating agents of the JRSO, and in accordance with an agreement reached at the time of the incorporation of the JRSO, the presidency and the chairmanship of the executive committee annually alternated between a representative of the JDC and a representative of the Jewish Agency for Palestine. Toward the end of 1948 the headquarters of the JRSO was established in Nuremberg. Jewish lawyers, who had been forced to flee from Germany, were recruited from all parts of the world to help search the records for evidence required to retrieve what had been illegally seized. On the basis of such evidence, thousands of claims were negotiated with current German possessors, or adjudicated by German administrative agencies and courts under the watchful eye of an American Appellate Tribunal. These proceedings encountered bitter opposition and hostility. The JRSO was forced to turn the bulk settlements over to the provincial governments as the only feasible means of expediting the recoveries. [Source: Ferencz, Benjamin. "Restitution to Nazi Victims- A Milestone in International Morality," from Two Generations in Perspective. Benjamin Ferencz Web Site, n.d. (14 April 2003).]

Beyond the immediate needs of housing and feeding the Jews who had survived, the JRSO began to formulate a plan as to how Germany would be held accountable and responsible for the devastation it had created. Even though one could not bring back the slaughtered millions, it was agreed upon that compensation was to be borne by the German people. Additionally, the theft of Jewish assets and properties had to be acknowledged and returned. In many cases, the properties and assets were stolen from families of which every member was murdered, leaving not a single survivor. That issue had to be addressed and a resolution found. In the end, although there would be no adequate moral or financial resolution, the Germans would be morally and financially burdened for years to come. But first, the Germans had to acknowledge that they were responsible for the European human catastrophe and take responsibility for it. Thus, it was that reparations, restitution and indemnification became the terms that were formulated for what the Germans would need to do. They would be obliged to pay for the damage they had perpetrated on the European Jews. Reparations, or Wiedergutmachungsabkommen in German, would provide monetary compensation for the survivors. Restitution required Germany to return the properties and assets they stole to their rightful owners. What was not returned required monetary compensation. Indemnification implied that the Germans would be held responsible for the future security of the Holocaust survivors.

The concept of reparations had no historical precedent. Thus, survivors and Jewish organizations needed to design a plan for compensation. The Germans dragged their feet for many years. After all, this was still a country of Nazis that showed no remorse. Their defeat did not change their moral decadence. The acknowledgement of their burden of responsibility changed when Konrad Adenaur became the Chancellor of West Germany in 1949. Adenaur, who was imprisoned for his opposition to the Nazi regime, conceded the wrongs of Nazi Germany and agreed to negotiate with representatives from Jewish organizations worldwide and with Israel. (Israel negotiated settlements with Germany independently). In the end, the European survivors would be represented by the Conference on Jewish Material Claims Against Germany, better known as the Claims Conference. The Claims Conference, the successor organization of JRSO, was established for the purposes of negotiating payments on behalf of survivors, distributing payments to survivors, providing social services to needy survivors and recovering property stolen from European Jews. However, until the establishment of the Claims Conference, the road to an agreement was replete with divergent interests, opinions, and political maneuverings that nearly undermined any resolution to a Jewish-German agreement.

The drama of restitution and reparations can be viewed from five angles: that of the Allies, the Germans, the worldwide Jewish community, the survivors and Israel. Because the angle of Israel has no bearing on my parents, it will not be discussed in this book.

The Allies

Germany, post-war, was divided into British, French, Soviet and American zones. Each zone was administered by these powers independently of one another. Thus, each zone had a different view on restitution and reparations for the Holocaust survivors. In other words, it was a mess with little consensus as to how to deal with the millions of Jews who were left destitute. There was even less agreement about how to compensate them for years of immeasurable deprivations, murders of their families, years of slave labor, torture and the theft of their personal and communal properties. Of the four allies, the United States was the most committed to righting the wrongs on behalf of the Holocaust survivors. Eventually, the British came around. Not to be ignored was the allies' concern about the economic impact the survivors would have on *their* countries' economies. Should Britain, France and the U.S. bear the economic brunt of the needs of the refugees and their resettlement? Or should the Germans?

Over time the political undercurrents shifted. The Soviet Union ceased being an ally and became an enemy of the West. Germany moved from being an enemy to an ally. With this turn of events, western countries reduced the pressure on Germany to help the Holocaust survivors. The United States Holocaust Memorial Museum website explains:

As the wartime alliance between East and West crumbled, United States policy toward Germany underwent drastic revision. Those who were formerly regarded as enemies were now sought as allies. This reversal brought with it a tendency to minimize the past. German pressure groups demanded the relinquishment of American controls and the abandonment of the restitution policy, but the attacks were successfully repelled. In the US Zone of occupation alone, property worth close to $250,000,000 was restored to former owners, now living in 60 different countries. In addition, heirless assets worth over $25,000,000 were recovered. These proceeds were used to provide shelter for refugees crowding tent camps in Israel, to aid needy Jews still living in Germany, hard-core medical cases, the aged, the blind and the destitute. [Source: Ferencz, Benjamin. "Restitution to Nazi Victims- A Milestone in International Morality," from Two Generations in Perspective. Benjamin Ferencz Web Site, n.d. (14 April 2003).]

Germany

Germany, after the war, was composed of the same anti-Semitic population it had before the war, but without fangs. With few exceptions, the Germans did not want to assume any financial burdens for what they had done. They felt that Germany was a country defeated and that the survivors were a burden. They preferred to ignore the billions of dollars in looted Jewish goods, assets and manufacturing that had enriched their country. Equally as maddening was the irony of the restitution and reparation issues. The Germans had made the theft of anything that Jews owned legal. After the war, they demanded proof from the Jews that the stolen property had been owned by them. Moreover, after their defeat, the Germans demanded the Jews go through *German* legal channels to prove that what Germans stole had belonged to its Jewish owners.

Fitting to the Nazis' mindset, the Germans did not wish to take into consideration the enormous Jewish human capital derived from the slave labor that benefitted their country. Why would they? This was a defeated country run by and consisting of the same Nazi supporters that had made genocide, theft, and murder legal. Ethics and morality had not been a part of the German makeup for many years so defeat would not suddenly cause that generation to soul search. Over time, the Germans would take responsibility for their wrongs. But the Holocaust survivors would be put through the ringer before that happened.

Jewish Organizations

During WWII, Jewish organizations began to plan for the needs of European Jewry once Germany was defeated. A considerable amount of money had been collected and then expended to help the Jews during and after the war. In the files of the American Jewish Joint Distribution Committee (JDC) is the following:

These relief efforts depicted in this collection encompassed JDC's extensive contributions to Palestine and then, after 1948, the State of Israel. JDC provided critical funding and supplies to the underground organized emigration effort to enable hundreds of thousands of Holocaust survivors to escape Eastern Europe to DP camps and Mediterranean seaports, and then subsequently to British Mandate Palestine.

After Israel became a state in 1948, its social services infrastructure was rapidly overwhelmed by waves of emigration, including many difficult-to-absorb populations such as the handicapped, elderly, and chronically ill immigrants. The following year, in 1949, JDC, in cooperation with the Jewish Agency for Israel and the Israeli government, created a social service organization called MALBEN. A year later, MALBEN operated entirely under the auspices of JDC to provide institutional care and social services; establish hospitals, clinics and old-age homes; train nurses and rehabilitation workers; and foster the development of private and public organizations in Israel for the care of the handicapped. As the Geneva records testify, the advent of MALBEN introduces the crucial role JDC played as a partner with the Israeli government in promoting comprehensive social welfare services and generating resources that addressed the needs of vulnerable populations in Israel.

After the war and during the dispersion of European Jewry into various countries around the world, Jewish organizations and the State of Israel pressed Germany to make financial amends to the survivors. In 1952, Germany, led by Conrad Adenauer, agreed to compensate the Holocaust survivors. The website for Claims Conference summarizes the arrangements as follows:

On September 10, 1952, after six months of negotiations, the Claims Conference and the West German federal government signed an agreement embodied in two protocols. Protocol No. 1 called for the enactment of laws that would compensate Nazi victims directly for indemnification (Sagi, 1986) and claims arising from Nazi persecution. Under Protocol No. 2, the West German government provided the Claims Conference with DM 450 million for the relief, rehabilitation and resettlement of Jewish victims of Nazi persecution, according to the urgency of their need as determined by the Conference. Agreements were also signed with the State of Israel.

The Survivors

Despite the 1952 agreement between Germany and worldwide Jewish organizations, the true story of reparations is long, complex and replete with years of struggles for many of the Holocaust survivors. Sadly enough, many of the Jews found themselves re-traumatized many times over in their attempts to receive reparations.

Soon after the war, there were rules and regulations as to who should be compensated. For instance, there was a period of time when only Jews who had been in concentration camps or in a ghetto for at least 18 months would be considered eligible for reparations. There was another eligibility requirement that the survivor had to prove that he or she suffered from a mental condition as a direct result of the Holocaust. Thus, a letter from a psychiatrist was required avowing that the survivor was mentally unstable. It was up to the survivor to *prove* his incarceration. It was up to the survivor to *prove* that he or she did not have a mental condition before the war. (This was a requirement despite the fact that those with mental illnesses were among the Nazis' first victims). Fleeing persecution, being in a ghetto, labor camp or concentration camp for 17 months or less did not count. Years of terror, the murder of family members, hiding from the murderers and their henchmen were irrelevant. Whatever roadblock the Germans could put up they did.

Then there was the bureaucracy. The bureaucracy the Germans erected to stymie Jewish claims was often insurmountable. Paperwork needed to be submitted, resubmitted and then re-resubmitted for any type of minutiae the Germans demanded. In this way, the Holocaust survivors would be tormented many times over if they wanted to be heard and have their claims validated.

The energy required by the Holocaust survivors to press for their claims was energy they needed to begin new lives, deal with the years of starvation and deprivation, accept that they were alive while the rest of their families had perished, and, importantly, to find a country where they could be safe and call home. There was little fortitude left to fight the Germans postwar.

Although my parents were not German, it is worth mentioning the distinct burdens of the German Jews who returned to their homeland. The Germans did not like nor want the German Jews to return, and when they did, they were treated as enemies rather than victims. As an additional onus, American and British soldiers subsumed the German Jews into the general German population. In effect, they were not considered to be displaced Jewish victims. Thus, funds to help the Jews from Poland, Hungary, Lithuania, Latvia, Greece, Romania, and Czechoslovakia were unavailable to German Jews.

Mom and Dad in the US

My parents were among the vast majority of Jews who refused to return to the countries from which they came, those same rabidly anti-Semitic countries whose populations had Jewish blood on their hands. Moreover, they had nobody and nothing left to return to. As a result, they either stayed in Germany or made their way to Germany. Germany, the country whose leaders and citizens had methodically destroyed European Jewry, became the primary transit zone for emigration out of Europe. After the war, Jews were safer in Germany than they would have been had they returned to Poland, Hungary, Czechoslovakia, Russia,

Lithuania and every other eastern European country. As proof, one need only refer to the pogrom in Kielce, Poland on July 4, 1946 where Polish soldiers, police and civilians brutally murdered 42 Jewish men, women and children who had returned to their city after surviving the Holocaust.

My parents applied for entry into the U.S. on August 17, 1948. My father's Refugee/Displaced Person Statistical Card showed that their eligibility status was for "Legal and political protection." My parents had also applied for immigration to Canada. My mother's sister had already immigrated there and had vouched for my parents. Just before they were set to leave for Canada and after a one-and-a-half-year wait, my parents were notified that they would be given entry into America. They came to the U.S. on January 6, 1950.

My mother and father were among the fortunate Holocaust survivors to be allowed entry into the United States. Gaining entry was difficult and complicated due to the requirements set up by the Immigration and Naturalization Services. There were strict limitations on the number of European Jews allowed to enter; most had to have a family member guarantee that the survivors would not be a burden on the economy. (In other words, said family member would agree to financially support the immigrants if needed). Additionally, those entering had to be in perfect physical and mental health.

Sadly enough, after all the survivors had been through, the visa limitations worked *against* the immigration of European Jewry. The consideration of what the war had done to the survivors received no sympathy from anti-Semitic power brokers and congressmen in Washington, D.C., who worked hard to allow as few Jews as possible to enter. Beth Cohen, in her book, *Case Closed: Holocaust Survivors in Postwar America*, highlights the numbers game that limited immigration and preserved the view that European Jews were not wanted. President Truman was sympathetic to the plight of the survivors but:

While Truman's words professed the humanitarian sentiment, in reality, the directive afforded only a minimal opportunity for the Jewish DPs to gain admittance. It allowed for the immigration each year of a maximum of 39,681 DPs into the United States from the American zones of occupation. Moreover, America admitted these newcomers within the quotas of the old immigration laws, which limited the number of visas according to the immigrant's country of origin. The directive was totally blind to the demographics of the Jewish DPs. The highest quota, for example, allowed 25,957 visas for Germans. There were barely 12,000 surviving German Jews in the American zones. By contrast, the directive set a quota of 6,524 for Poland, which was far below the number of Polish survivors. An estimated 28,000 Jewish DPs entered America by June 1948 as a result of the new policy. More than 90 percent of these were on quota.[1]

In April 1948, the House of Representatives passed the Fellows Bill allowing 100,000 DPs a year for two years. As the plight of the Jewish DPs continued, the Senate, on June 2, 1948 voted for the Wiley-Rivercomb Bill. This bill further restricted survivor immigration into the United States. With this bill in place, 50,000 DPs a year would be allowed to immigrate but only for two years. Cohen writes of the Wiley-Rivercomb Bill:

Clearly biased against Jewish DPs, it demanded not only that 50 percent of admitted DPs be farmers but also gave preference to those from the Baltic region. There were few farmers and few surviving Balts among the Jewish DPs; that was the area with the greatest number of Protestant DPs.

The Wiley-Rivercomb Bill also stipulated a cutoff date. In order to be eligible to enter the United States, one had to have been in Germany, Austria or Italy before 22 December 1945. This was the kiss of death for Jewish DP immigration, because the majority had entered these countries after that date.[2]

On June 25, 1948, President Truman signed the Displaced Persons Act. About the Displaced Persons Act Cohen writes that it, "…combined the worst features of the two competing bills." The cutoff date of the Wiley-Rivercomb Bill remained, 30 percent of the visas would be given to agricultural workers and 40 percent would be given to immigrants of Baltic extraction. In the end, nearly 140,000 survivors immigrated to America."

Unfortunately, anti-Semitism was built into the fabric of American society at the time. Nor did it help that, among some American Jews, there was the underlying fear that an influx of survivors would cause anti-Semitism to increase and would therefore affect their personal comfort. Then there were the Zionists who pressed for the creation of the State of Israel and for the immigration of European Jewry to the new Jewish state.

---

[1] Cohen, Beth B., Case Closed (New Brunswick: Rutgers University Press, 2007), p. 14.

[2] Ibid.

The American Jewish community deserves no kudos in other matters as well. When talking about his arrival in the United States, my father would always remember to tell me about a Jewish co-worker on his first job in New York. The man was resentful that an immigrant got a job that should have gone to an American. He never cared that my father had survived nor showed any sympathy whatsoever. Such was my father's first experience in the U.S. My parents said that American Jewry, overall, showed little interest in the survivors. With the exception of the Hebrew Immigration Aid Society (HIAS), my parents got no assistance from Jewish organizations or individuals. From HIAS, my parents received diapers (I was born about six weeks after they arrived) and basic household items. Other than HIAS assistance, my parents were on their own. We knew many survivors but knew of none who received help from American Jews. My dad's family member, who signed as a guarantor, slipped out of my parents' lives once they arrived in New York. I never met her. My mother had an uncle, Shiya, who had 11 children whose sons all become lawyers or judges. Except for one daughter, none were in our lives, and she only briefly. I recall that she invited my parents to her son's bar mitzvah. My parents were introduced to my mother's first cousins, who, after the introductions, moved on, never to be seen again. Such was the welcome my parents received from family and American Jewry. It is no wonder that my father always said that he and my mother made it on their own, with help from no one. My aunts and uncles received no help from American Jews, nor did any survivors I knew throughout my life. I had an acquaintance in Phoenix, Toby, whose father survived the war and landed in New Orleans, where he raised his family. Toby and I were once talking about the experiences of our parents vis a vis the American Jewish community. Her father had told her that American Jews gave no support, financial or otherwise, to their European brethren when they arrived in the States. Leo, another child of Holocaust survivors, and his family arrived in the U.S., from Israel in the 1960s. However, his aunt who arrived in U. S. in 1946, told of wealthy family members who did not offer help of any kind.

As stated before, the Jews of Europe would quickly learn that they were on their own. For the most part, they were the unwelcome guests at the American Jewish party. Despite the fact that this knowledge was shared by the majority of survivors, Cohen, in *Case Closed: Holocaust Survivors in Postwar America*, noted that there were a few lucky survivors whose experience was positive. However, even they knew that they were a small minority.

But a recurring theme among them is also the sentiment that they were among the lucky minority in contrast to other newcomers. They reiterate the belief that deeply positive mutual feelings between the survivors and American Jewish relatives were rare. The pattern that emerges from both the case files and oral histories supports this contention. It reflects a range from limited help to outright indifference to active rejection. After all, 90 percent of the immigrants who came to New York through family sponsorship turned to NYANA [New York Association for New Americans] for assistance.

The attitude of American Jews to the survivors piqued my interest as I was writing this story. There are not many elderly American Jews still alive to ask about this time period. A friend's mother, now in her 90s, but whose memory and mind are intact, was in her 20s during WWII. She grew up in the Bronx until she was 13, when her parents moved to a small town in the Catskills. When she was ready to attend college she returned to Manhattan, where she lived with her aunt in the 1940s and 1950s. She said that she knew nothing about what was happening to the Jews in Germany prior to WWII nor to European Jewry during the war. She began to hear about the horrors of the Holocaust in the late 1940s. It was not until she moved to Phoenix in 1994 that she met a survivor.

I have known Isabel since I was three years old. She is now in her 90s. She and her husband, Jerry, were born and raised in America. They met my parents when we moved to Newark, New Jersey, in 1953. I asked Isabel when she had first learned that my parents were Holocaust survivors. She related the following to me: She had returned to her apartment complex when she looked up at a window next to her apartment. In the window she saw a striped garment hanging out to dry. She immediately knew that her new neighbors were survivors. She did not talk to them about it at the time. She wrote the following to me in an email, "Your parents hardly talked about their war experiences while we lived in Newark. However, once they moved to Arizona they spoke freely. Your mother seemed to be very traumatized...still."

Barbara Burstin, in her article "Holocaust Survivors: Rescue and Resettlement in the United States," focused primarily on the volunteer work of the National Council of Jewish Women (NCJW) and the experiences of women Holocaust survivors in the Pittsburgh area. The NCJW women assisted the survivors by taking them to appointments, helping them find housing and providing clothing and household goods. Burstin notes, "Yet, despite the efforts of NCJW women, there was still a distance between them and the newcomers that was keenly felt by the refugee women. NCJW volunteers did not provide the friendship and warmth that many of the survivors of the Holocaust needed. Americans, both men and women, did not understand or appreciate what these 'greeners' had been through, and the survivors soon learned, if they had been so inclined, not to talk about their experiences except among themselves. Ethel Landerman, a young social work intern for Montefiore Hospital where the refugees were treated free of charge, remarked: 'We had no sense of the Holocaust as we know now, with a capital H. We really didn't understand what people were telling us. The stories sounded too horrible. We simply did not believe them.' The women survivors associated with one another. They met in the park with their children."

There is no doubt that the survivors, like most immigrants who came to America throughout the years, found comfort and camaraderie among those who, like them, had survived. Yet, for survivors there was the added burden of horrors that were impossible for non-survivors to begin to grasp. The incomprehensibility of the horrors sometimes led non-survivors to ask survivors questions that were at best ignorant and at worst made the victims feel as if *they* had done something wrong. One of the common questions asked was why did the survivors not fight back? I am guilty of having asked my parents that when I was young. Fight back, they would ask with a sarcastic chuckle? How were we supposed to fight back? With what? An entire nation of armed Poles didn't last but a few days. The question disgusted them.

Dorothy Rabinowitz, in her book *New Lives: Survivors of the Holocaust Living in America*, interviewed several survivors about their war and post war experiences. One female survivor, Elena, recounted, "You understand, the concentration camp experience is nothing that endears you to people. People who came to my cousin's house used to ask me such things as whether I had been able to survive because, perchance, I had slept with an SS man." Then there was the experience of Emil. He had attended meetings with social workers and psychiatric counselors but, within a short time, became resentful of their "superior air" and "psychological queries" and "probing personal questions." He came to loathe their sense of superiority. One psychiatric counselor asked him if he felt guilty about surviving. After Emil shook his head no, the counselor persisted to probe, "I mean guilt about survival; you don't feel upset from time to time that other people in your family died and that you lived? That's what the question means. Now do you feel guilty about this sometimes?" Another survivor had the unpleasant experience of being told by an American-born Jew, "You have a terrific imagination," after she had heard about gas chambers. One survivor had a man, seeing the tattooed numbers on her forearm, ask her, "I was wondering why you were wearing your laundry numbers on your arm." He wanted to know if they were some kind of decoration. She replied that they were her telephone number. She later learned that the man was the dean of a law school.

There was a litany of other questions commonly asked of survivors that irritated them into silence. One such question was, "Why did you survive?" Some Americans felt they understood the years of starvation that the survivors endured because there had been shortages of food in America during the war. There were American Jews who showed no interest in knowing about the survivor's experience. Rabinowitz analyzes this approach by stating, "This was a generous attitude, but one that also served to isolate those survivors who could not successfully pretend that the had been nowhere, and that nothing of significance had happened to them in the five years or more that they had spent in captivity or hiding." Another interviewee, Sarah, avoided talking about starvation, the ghetto, Auschwitz, selections and other horrid events because she felt that Americans would not believe events that were so incredibly sordid. In other words, one could not understand events that were beyond comprehension unless one had been there. In *Case Closed: Holocaust Survivors in Postwar America*, Cohen underlines the critical component in the survivors' silence:

Moreover, it is generally accepted that survivors would not or could not speak then about their painful memories and instead endeavored to put the past behind them as they moved forward. Contemporary documents voice exactly the opposite. The survivors had much to say, but their listeners were deaf to what the survivors had to tell them. [3]

I need to mention the group of Americans who understood well what happened to the European Jews: the soldiers who had entered the concentration camps. I remember speaking to an American veteran who had liberated a camp. I told him that my parents were survivors. His expression turned to anguish and he began to cry. He told me that he could not talk about what he had seen. He never told his wife or children what he witnessed. Rabinowitz cites the experience of a survivor who happened to meet a veteran of WWII in his small men's store. The veteran noticed the numbers tattooed on the survivor's arm. The veteran remarked, "Oh, I see you got your souvenir. Well, don't try to tell people here what happened over in Europe; forget about it. I was in the American Army. I walked into those camps and I saw all those things the Germans did, and people here don't believe it when you tell them." The vet added that he stopped talking about the war to anybody who had not been a witness to its horrors.

---

[3] Cohen, Beth B., Case Closed (New Brunswick: Rutgers University Press, 2007), p. 132.

Fortunately, the survivors were, for the most part, an ambitious, hardy and independent group. Despite their hardships and chilly reception into the "goldenah landt" (the golden land), as it was referred to by survivors, this country offered them the opportunities to make their dreams come true. As the years went on, my parents took incredible pride in their accomplishments, those of their children and of survivors. The children of survivors became lawyers, doctors, engineers, teachers, and an array of other professionals. All this from people who were marked for death, who defied the Nazis' attempts at extermination and who came to America penniless.

Reparations — Years of Struggle

My parents were among the survivors for whom receiving reparations was replete with years of struggle, frustration, and roadblocks. I recall my parents complaining about the hoops they had to jump through. Right after the war, my father was told that he had to get a letter from a psychiatrist stating that he was no longer mentally sound as a result of his incarceration in concentration camps. I recall my father angrily saying that he was not going to say that he was crazy to get the payments. My aunt, on the other hand, went along with the demand and received money. My mother was automatically considered ineligible because she had not been in a concentration camp. Nor had she been in a ghetto for at least eighteen months. After the war, when in Germany, she decided to tell the authorities that she had been in a camp in order to receive reparations since her version of the German horror show did not count. Somehow, they found out that she had not been in a concentration camp. She was blacklisted from ever receiving reparations. This would be the beginning of endless obstacles awaiting my parents as they attempted to get monetary compensation for their years of suffering, loss of their families and loss of their youth.

Establishing claims did not get easier for my parents once the Claims Conference was established in 1952. At that time, my parents had been in the U.S. two years and their English was rudimentary. Additionally, they had a child, me, and had to work. There were no handouts for food, clothing or rent. They, like many other survivors, did not have the time or, they believed, the skills to slog through the process of getting compensation. My father had little to no patience for tasks that involved reading details, following up on sources, filling out applications and the minutiae required in the application requests. My mother had the patience for the task but easily gave up if she was told that she was ineligible. She did not have the personality to fight for her rights. Thus, my parents came to select a different avenue available to press for claims.

In the 1950's, there arose, out of the survivor establishment, those Jews who felt themselves prepared to represent the survivors when they applied for claims. Survivors paid these representatives to advise them, do the necessary reparation paperwork, and oversee their application process. The survivors paid for the services out of their own pockets. I remember one such man, Mr. Urbach, who represented my parents, aunt, uncle, and perhaps other survivors with whom we lived in Newark, New Jersey. He represented my parents sometime between 1953 and 1958.

I cannot say what Mr. Urbach did or did not do for my parents. However, years later, I talked to my parents about reparations. I wondered why they were not receiving compensation. My father told me that, at one point, he had the option of receiving a lump sum payment or monthly payments. He opted to take a lump sum payment of about $8,000. My mother was not receiving compensation because she was on the German blacklist for lying.

Years later, when my niece visited the U.S. Holocaust Memorial Museum in Washington, D. C., she requested information on my parents. Among the copies of paperwork were letters, written on behalf of my father and mother. These short letters demonstrated the purposeless and continual struggles that my parents were subjected to in their quest to receive reparations. The first letter in the packet was written on November 30, 1957, to the International Search Service. It was written by someone named Hupe. The letter stated, "Since more than 10 months since my inquiry to you have passed and the representative (guardian?) of the applicant pushes for quick compensation, I ask you to process my request from 30.1.1957 with priority, so that the applicant can receive financial aid soon. The application is ready for a decision." My parents never received a decision. On March 10, 1978, again a letter was sent to the International Search Service. This time it was on behalf of my mother and father and written by L. Kozeminski. It stated, "For the two above mentioned persons I would like to ask you again to find out, where and in which decision-making office those two cases are located and are processed." On March 31, 1978, A. Opitz, Leader of the Archives, replied to Kozeminski, "To answer your above mentioned letter, we inform you that the compensation cases of the above mentioned were processed by the regional president of Hannover under the document code –EB-IB/PR-1 24 353-G- and –EB-IV/E-1 25 243-G-. We hope, we have helped you with this information." Then, on May 18, 1996, G. Wilke from the County office of Lower Saxony wrote a letter regarding the ongoing inquiries. The letter was "for sustenance and care? –Compensation-," on behalf of my father. Wilke wrote, "Ladies and Gentlemen! The former request can now be supplemented based on the newly received documentation. Should there be other information necessary for the above case, we ask for a brief message. We will then start the Analysiss [sic] of the newly received Materials in relation to the incarceration and let you know the result. Otherwise we will view the case as taken care of." I have no idea what Wilke did or did not do. I just know that nothing came of my parents' attempts to receive compensation.

I recall that at one point in the 1960s when I was in either middle or high school, my parents were contacted by someone, or they contacted someone they had heard about, who reopened survivor reparation cases through the German courts. He had contacts with German lawyers who supposedly fought for reparations through the German courts. I remember my parents paying this man, but nothing ever came of it. This further underlined their belief that attempting to get compensation was futile. Years later, I believe it was in the latter part of the 1980s, they tried again. Again, reparations eluded them.

In the late 1990s, I decided to become involved in my parents' rights to reparations. By this time, the German government had agreed to widen the scope of who could qualify to receive compensation. Nevertheless, my parents were not optimistic about their chances, but they cooperated with me as I decided to battle my way through the German and Claims Conference bureaucratic barriers.

My first battle was to get reparations for my parents. I contacted lawyers in the Washington, D.C., area who had gotten involved in Holocaust reparations. They agreed to take on my father's case. The American lawyers worked with German lawyers to represent my father. It was a process that would take a few years but eventually they succeeded in getting my father a large lump sum payment and monthly reparations that would last until his death in 2011. They also succeeded in getting monthly reparations for my mother.

Later, when I learned that monthly German social security benefits were due to those who worked for Germany within German annexed territory at any time (Lodz was annexed during WWII), I applied for my father. My father was thrilled when his monthly benefits began.

The last of my attempts to receive a modicum of compensation for the losses of my parents occurred when the Swiss admitted that they had stashes of gold stolen from the Jews. My maternal grandfather had frequent dealings with Switzerland when it came to watches. When the Germans entered Lwow, in 1941, they confiscated everything in his store. I made the claim on this basis. My mother received money from the Swiss.

Needless to say, monetary compensation of any kind is a lame substitute for what happened to my parents. But if it made their lives easier in any way, these payments were worth fighting for. It is a pity that they had to struggle to receive monetary compensation at all.

Trip to Poland

In 1999, my daughter, Keren, took a trip to Poland with the International March of the Living. Each year this group brings individuals from around the world to Poland and Israel to study the history of the Holocaust and to examine the roots of prejudice, intolerance and hatred.

Keren

Snow crunched under the 20 pairs of shoes that alighted. One step outside and the numbness I had felt throughout Poland swept into my body again. The cold froze every bone and muscle in my body. I walked through the large concrete and metal building, wondering when I would see the horror, hoping I would see it because although I had been to the Warsaw ghetto, seen the human ashes at Majdanek, I had felt no emotions surge through my body as I had expected. I looked at my watch—four more hours until I would leave for warm Israel. Four hours left to make myself understand what my grandfather went through. My group walked through the barracks. Pictures of prisoners stared at me. I stared back to see if I recognized them. We walked past the room of suitcases. I looked to see if I could find a name I recognized. We stood before the roll call area, a vast expanse of snow-covered space. Without any pictures to relate to, I focused on wiggling my toes to get some feeling back in them. Two hours until I left for Israel and Auschwitz seemed empty—devoid of the horrors that made it famous — and my mind felt empty—unable to place my grandfather in this place. We walked to the gas chambers. It was my last chance to cry—when I would realize what my grandfather went through. Inside the gas chambers someone pointed out the fingernail scratches in the concrete wall. My body went numb.

I left the group and walked outside, determined to feel the weight and meaning of Auschwitz. Deep inside the Auschwitz gas chamber Mirla, Chaya and Yossel huddled together shaking as the poison gas began to pour out of the showerheads. Screams surrounded them. Did they scream? Women piled onto one another to find a hole in the door with fresh air. Women scratched the concrete walls, scratching their fingernails to bloody shreds as if they could claw themselves out. One by one, each succumbed to the gas. They began to seize and convulse as the poison cruelly wrapped itself around their lungs, entering their bloodstreams. Jewish women lay in motionless heaps, little Yossel among them.

My grandfather marched past the chamber of death into Birkenau. My friend came over to me and put her hand on my shoulder. The tears fell.

Mirla

The priests of Poland railed against the Jews to their congregations while the laws of Poland discriminated against them. Instead of protecting the Jews, the police blamed them. If a Jew was attacked by Poles and had the audacity to fight back, the Jew was arrested. Jewish men were forced into military service, where they were treated as second-class citizens and were denigrated by the anti-Semitic Polish soldiers they served beside.

They were citizens of a country that not only did not protect them during WWII, but eagerly denounced them to the German invaders. Thus, it came as no surprise to the Jews that the Polish government, Polish Catholic Church and the Polish people turned away from them after the German invasion. At best, they ignored what the Germans were doing to the Jews. At worst, they were complicit by pointing out the Jews to the Germans, squealing about a hidden Jew's whereabouts or killing the Jews themselves. There were Poles who, for gold, jewelry, or other valuables would hide a Jew. When the money ran out or the Jew was unable to furnish more valuables, the Poles ran to the Germans to rat the Jew out. Many took pleasure in watching the Germans torment an innocent Jew on the street. This country of devout Catholics was not happy with the German invasion except for the fact that the Nazis would cleanse the country of Jews. The Jewish people, who each Sunday the Catholic priests demonized and spewed hatred towards, would be gone from their country once and for all. The Jews of Poland lived with this hatred on a daily basis before, during and after the war. Except for a small number, who are now called Righteous Gentiles, the Jews worst fears came true—their countrymen would not be there for them and they hated them back for that. There were few survivors who would want to set foot again into the country of their birth. Neither my parents, aunts, uncle nor their friends ever wanted to be in Poland again. I was aware of the strong feelings my parents had towards Poland and the Poles. Yet, I had a strong desire to see where my parents lived and grew up. My family's roots had been ripped out and mostly destroyed. The physical roots of their lives might still be intact. I wanted to see where they lived, worked, played, prayed, and breathed.

It was no easy task to convince my parents to return to Poland. I worked on them for many months before I was finally able to convince them to return with me. I planned the trip in detail: where we would go, where we would stay and how we would get around. We would be in Poland a week. During that time, we would go to Lodz, Krakow, Auschwitz, possibly Lwow and then back to Warsaw for a couple of days before flying to Israel. I reserved rooms at the Holiday Inns in Warsaw and Krakow and at the Grand Hotel in Lodz. My parents knew a

Jewish couple who had traveled to Poland a year or two earlier. They recommended that we hire a driver.

Summer of 1990

As the departure date of our trip neared, I became increasingly worried about my parents. Had I done the right thing by convincing them to return to the country where they had lost their beloved families, homes and nearly their lives? Would the trip be too traumatic for them? What would happen to them emotionally? It worried me tremendously.

I left my husband and two young children, whom we were to meet up with in Israel, and flew, with my parents, to New York. From there we boarded the Polish airline, LOT, to Warsaw. Shortly into the flight, the flight attendants began the liquor service. I think we were some of the few passengers who did not drink. The passengers went from subdued to loud, happy and boisterous. A few hours later, all were asleep, except for me.

We arrived in Warsaw sometime in mid-morning. We departed the plane by staircase onto the tarmac and walked a short distance to a decrepit terminal. We passed through the Polish entry controls. My mom and I went to use the bathroom while my dad waited for our luggage. I waited outside of the stall, by the sink, in a dilapidated bathroom. From the stall, I heard my mom say that there was no toilet paper. I looked around for paper towels and saw none. As I glanced around the room, I noticed the toilet paper, suspended on a nail about six feet above the floor. I thought this could be fodder for another stupid Polish joke. At least I could reach it. It would have been way beyond my five-foot-tall mother's reach had I gone in the stall first.

After gathering our luggage, we hired a driver to take us from the airport to our hotel. The Holiday Inn was an American oasis in the bleak gray Warsaw landscape. Everything about the city was depressing — its ugly gray drab Communist-inspired block buildings devoid of any architectural aesthetic, the dour faces of the Poles, and the poverty of the city around us. I noticed how quiet it was, as if the joy, vivacity, and excitement of a big city had been sucked out by a great tsunami, leaving a cloud of dreariness and depression in its wake.

After settling into our room, my dad and I headed to the front of the hotel to find a driver for the week. Drivers were lined up next to their cars waiting for passengers. Dad approached a driver and, in Polish, asked him if he was interested in a job as our driver for a few days. They talked about the price. Dad then approached two more drivers. Curiously, the price of each subsequent driver increased from that of the previous driver's quote. I watched the interactions from a distance and became increasingly uncomfortable with what I was observing. Each driver watched my dad and as my dad moved on, he made eye contact with the driver my dad had just left. Finally, my dad made arrangements with one driver to come by the next morning to begin our trip through Poland.

I was unable to relax enough to fall asleep that night. Fortunately, my parents had no trouble and woke up the next morning refreshed. I, on the other hand, had not slept since leaving Arizona two days earlier. Some people can function fairly normally on little to no sleep. I, instead, become a basket case. I lose my appetite, become weepy and feel ill. So here I was, starting my journey through Poland as a bundle of nerves.

My parents had breakfast, as I sat there, a bundle of nerves unable to down a bite. My dad and I went to the hotel lobby and waited for the driver. As the time passed for him to arrive, my paranoia increased. What if the driver were to take us to a deserted area and physically harm us? What if he were to take us somewhere, rob us, and leave us to find our way back? Totally irrational, I know, but those were my thoughts on no sleep or food. Finally, unable to take it anymore, I told my dad that I did not want to travel around Poland with a Polish driver. I suggested that we consider renting a car. My dad agreed and we immediately made our way over to the hotel's car rental desk. An hour later, our luggage was squeezed into the back of our ultra-small red rental car and we were off. I was relieved to be alone with my parents and not have to think about whether the driver was an anti-Semite who might do something cruel to us.

Our first destination was Lodz, about a two-hour-drive southeast of Warsaw. Our goal was to arrive before noon. The drive was going smoothly until we approached a small village where we encountered a huge traffic jam. Cars were jammed together and horns were blaring. I was certain that there was some terrible accident up ahead. We asked a pedestrian who was crossing the street what was going on. She told us that there was a nationwide truckers' strike; the truckers were blocking all major arteries in the entire country. We were stuck. Then I noticed that some drivers were beginning to use the sidewalks as alternatives to the jammed street. Perhaps they knew a way around the jam. I followed them. A half-mile of sidewalk and shoulder driving brought us to the front of the mess. Trucks and plows were stretched across the road blocking all traffic. It was impossible to pass and there were no alternative routes since all were made impassable by the striking truckers. Fortunately, we were stopped in front of a roadside restaurant. We decided to have an early lunch, hoping that, by the time we had finished eating, the strike would be over. My father was anxious to get to Lodz and head straight for the Jewish cemetery, where his father and brother were buried. Eager to get to Lodz, we finished our meals and left the restaurant only to find traffic still at a standstill.

Suddenly, I felt extremely uncomfortable to be surrounded by Poles. As we walked towards the crowds, I asked my parents to only speak English. The reason was that I was worried that if my parents spoke Polish that somehow the Poles would discern that we were Jewish and would then harm us. Such was my paranoia. Perhaps it was my lack of sleep playing with my emotional state. Perhaps it was knowing how the Jews in Poland had been treated as Polish citizens. I went over to my mom and told her about my fears. She looked at me as if there were something wrong with me and said, "Don't be ridiculous. These people won't hurt you. They're harmless." At that moment, I felt the emotional weight vaporize. Here I was, surrounded by Poles, and my mother said I had nothing to worry about.

I watched my parents as we merged into the groups of people milling around. My parents looked so different from the Poles. The way they dressed set them apart from the locals; my parents looked American and cosmopolitan. The clothing the Poles wore looked drab in contrast to my parents' stylishness. The difference was striking and made me feel proud. These were the Jews the Poles threw out of their country and look how far they had come in America.

We learned that the strike was to last four hours. We had three more hours to stand around and wait. People were milling around and talking. A drunkard approached us and began speaking in Polish. We looked at him and said, "English. America." He continued to speak to us in Polish, inviting us to come have tea with him at his house. True to our pact to speak only English, we did not answer him. My mom and I chuckled as we spoke to each other about the invitation. As he was leaving, he said something to my mother. She answered him in Polish. He looked at her and said, "You speak Polish!" Playing dumb, my mother reverted back to English. The drunk turned to a farmer nearby and excitedly told him that we speak Polish. The young farmer looked at us as the drunk returned to me and insisted, in Polish, that we come for tea. A policeman walked over and asked what was going on. The young farmer told him that the drunkard was hearing things and would not leave me alone. The policeman turned to the drunk and suggested that he go home and sleep it off. To our surprise, we soon achieved celebrity status. A news reporter learned that there were Americans among the crowd. She made her way over to us and, in English, asked if we would mind being interviewed about the strike. We said okay. She asked us where we were from, where we were headed, what we thought of the strike. As she was interviewing us, a busload of Japanese tourists pulled up on the other side of the barricade. They disembarked with their cameras. They moved along through the crowd snapping pictures of what had now become a surreal scene. The Americans were being interviewed for the Polish news as the Japanese were capturing it all on film.

The strike finally ended at exactly the four-hour point. Everyone was anxious to get on their way. We got in our little red car and inched towards the moving barrier. As the trucks moved away, we saw someone in the middle of the road directing traffic—it was the drunk. He saw us, stopped traffic in both directions, and with a smile waved good-bye.

Lodz

The trucker's strike, unfortunately, had cost us the day in Lodz. By the time we arrived at the Grand Hotel, it was about five in the evening. I reserved our rooms there because it was the best hotel I could find in the city. This had been the best hotel in Lodz before the war. Time and neglect had stripped it of its prior beauty. The inside was dreary, unkempt and dour, with furnishings that were old and worn out. Our room was equally depressing. The beds were old, the wallpaper was peeling and the carpet was tattered and stained.

We agreed that it was probably too late to visit the cemetery. Instead, my father and I decided to go for a walk while my mother rested. We walked along the two-lane main street, Ulica (Street) Pietrowska, the grandest avenue in pre-war Lodz. My dad was taken aback by the condition of the buildings and the derelict look of the surroundings. He told me that this had once been an elegant area where only the wealthy could afford to live or shop. The buildings on Ulica Pietrowska had retained their architectural baroque style but their drabness and decaying appearances belied their grandiose past. My dad noted the change with satisfaction; the Poles deserved to live like this after the way they mistreated the Jews.

Before the war this was the main street in Lodz. There were businesses, the most elegant businesses. It was equivalent to let's say Fifth Avenue in New York. It was a mainly Jewish section. A lots of Jewish people lived here. The winter of 1939, they surrounded blocks in the night. They made the Jews leave and leave behind all their belongings.

We looked through a tunnel-like structure. Behind it were a building on the left, right and directly opposite us, surrounding a courtyard in the middle.

This is a typical tenement housing where you consisted of a house in front with a yard surrounded by houses on the left, right and the rear. We lived in a similar house.

There were not many people walking around Poland's second largest city and, like Warsaw, it was eerily quiet. The only noise we heard came from what sounded like a scuffle on a corner lot nearby. There was a group of men watching two men shouting at each other. My father insisted that we leave. He said they were probably drunk and that it would not take too long before the two would begin hitting each other and then everyone else would join in.

On our way back to the hotel, we came upon a couple of boys who looked to be about seven or eight. My dad pulled out a couple of candy bars he had brought from the States and handed one to each boy. We had not gone far before the two boys returned with some friends who also wanted candy. How had my dad known to bring candy? There, on Ulica Pietrowska, my dad, the survivor, emptied out his pockets for the poor boys of Lodz. We returned to the hotel, had dinner and prepared for an early night. Our first destination the next morning would be the area of the Jewish ghetto and my dad's home on 59 Ulica Franciskynska.

Former Ghetto Area

We arrived at Baluty Rinek. Baluty Rinek was the site of the outdoor market where my grandmother would do much of her shopping. This area abutted the poorest section of Lodz. I tried to picture my grandmother shopping here but that was not possible since I did not know what she looked like. For some reason I could not picture my dad or uncle walking the streets either. I could not establish a concrete reference point in my mind.

Once the Germans entered Lodz, Baluty Rinek was established as the frontline of the Lodz Ghetto.

When the Germans established the ghetto, this was their administration. From here they administered the activities of the ghetto. And the buildings they put up, the buildings are no more here. Where the marketplace is, there was the administration. From here, the Jews, in the

143

beginning, they shipped out. On this side was the administration and there was a gate to the other side. And in other words, this was separation. One side, one gate, led to the Balutsky Rinek administration and the other gate was out from the ghetto. This [where we stood] was the middle of the ghetto. All this was part of the ghetto. The building that you see here [newer buildings with balconies] *all the new buildings were built after the war. The ghetto was surrounded by barbed wire. They're no more in existence.*

As we stood on the corner where the ghetto once was, I saw a low wooden structure with a pitched roof. I asked my dad if that building typified prewar Lodz.

This typical building that you see on your left you could find all over the ghetto. This part of the ghetto some buildings are new and probably some are old.

We looked around us at mostly dilapidated buildings. Before us was one of them.

The building, a brick building, in the ghetto which is still in existence. That's the corner of Lnarska and Zawishy Charnega (two main streets).

We continued walking.

The buildings are all from the ghetto. This is Lnarska and the cross street is Vlade Vitomske (another street).

We continued walking until we reached Ulica Franciskynska. My father had a hard time finding the building where he lived. When he lived there as a boy, the apartment building was fronted by a wooden house and courtyard. We looked at the building numbers. We arrived in front of a light brownish grayish building that had grass in front and trees that obscured some of windows from the street. We moved closer—59 Franciskyanska was still standing! So, this was where my father lived. The wooden house and courtyard were gone. The building was old, had areas of fallen plaster and needed to be painted. However, it was not as dilapidated as other buildings in the area. The apartment building was four stories high. To the left of the entrance there were four windows the breadth of the left side. To the right of the entrance the windows were five abreast. A couple of the panes were broken. Below each window sat a shelf where one could put a pie to cool or flowerpots. In front of the building, a dog was walking on the grass and sniffing around. It felt surreal to be standing in front of the building where my father grew up and where my grandparents, aunts and uncles once lived.

This is the building that me and my family lived here. That is 59 Franciskyanska. I grew up here. I spent my years, the war years in the ghetto, I spent here til we left. Til the Germans discovered us, we were hiding here. And they shipped us, me, my mother, my sister, the older sister, and two brothers, they shipped us to Auschwitz. And that was one day, August the 27ᵗʰ. That was the last day that we spent in the ghetto.

We lived in the building facing us. The lower floor on the left-hand side of the entrance that was the woodworking shop, with the red window. All sides, all windows my father occupied as a woodworking shop. On the second floor there was a synagogue, a shtiebel. On the third floor, we lived on the third floor. On the fourth floor on the left-hand side, if you'll move over, I'll tell you who lived there. Go a little bit farther. Those windows lived a family and their name was Chazen with five children. Next to it were Weister with two children, a boy and a girl and they lived on the right-hand side. And they all perished during the war. On the other side of the building, there lived a family, Greenberg, with two children. Their name was Anon and Aren. Then next to the window, lived a family Weinberg. They're a family of five. They all perished during the war. Below the whole floor was occupied by a family Greenberg. They were a family of seven. Only one son survived, Yoyich. He went to Russia and that's how he survived. On the second floor, the whole second floor, on the right, was landlord and the name was Tischler. His son, before the war, disappeared. Apparently, he went to Germany. When the Germans entered, he came back dressed in a black uniform. He became an SS man. He was a German, an SS man. The first floor, there was a woodworking shop, and this was, this belonged to a family, Bend and Leibish. They were partners. In the basement, my father kept his lumber. The second floor, the fourth window. Between the fourth window and the third was divided, the apartment, with a wall. We hid in the last room during the last aktion, when they were sending out, the final solution, they sent out the Jews. There was an entrance to the last room. We took a closet and put it against the wall. There were books on the bottom. We took out the shelf and we crawled in and we hid there. The ghetto was almost empty and the Germans discovered us in this room. And from this room we went, my mother, my two sisters, my sister's boy, Leibel (Uncle Leo) with his wife and the family. The Germans discovered us. They discovered us, the family we hid with us, he (one of the men of the other family hiding with them) went down on Zhavisa to see something and the German officer, he stopped him. And he said he want his family with him. So, when he came to get his family they discovered us. From here they took us to Auschwitz.

My dad and I passed through the double doors at the entrance to the building. My father pointed to a door on the right directly behind the front door. It was about five feet high.

This door led to a basement. And during the gheshperre we used to hide underneath.

As my dad was telling me about the basement door, a man walked towards the building entrance. He looked to be about 60 years old. He was balding, wore glasses and a jacket over a striped shirt. My parents began to talk to him. As they talked, I stood in front of the door to my grandfather's woodworking shop and then made my way up the dark stairwell arriving at the front door of my dad's apartment. It was surreal. This was the door that my grandparents, aunts and uncles passed through every day. Now there I was. I stood there trying to picture my family coming out and going in through that door. I tried to picture my grandmother opening the door and happily greeting me, but I could not. I knocked on the door, not knowing what I would say if someone were to open it. No answer. I knocked again. No answer. I was somewhat relieved because I felt nervous and awkward. I rejoined my parents and took one last look at the building.

The next morning, we set out to visit the gravesites of my grandfather Itzhak and Uncle Hirsch. The receptionist at the Grand Hotel gave us directions to the cemetery. She informed us that it was overgrown and not taken care of so that we would have a hard time finding it. We followed her directions to the area. We could not find the cemetery. We stopped to ask a pedestrian. She pointed in the direction of weeds and overgrowth. We asked her where the entrance was. She told us she was not sure. We drove in the area around the cemetery but could not find the entrance. We stopped. We looked. We drove. We did this for the entire morning. No matter which direction we drove, we could not find the entrance. The exploration was frustrating, especially for my father. He so badly wanted to visit his father's and brother's graves.

Close to noon I started to get nervous. I had made reservations for that night at the Holiday Inn in Krakow. I wanted to get there before 6 pm so as not to lose our room. There was no way to call the hotel to tell them we may be late and to hold the room. In 1990, Poland's telephone system was in the dark ages. All calls had to go through an operator. Because there were a limited number of available lines, the operator would call the caller when a line became available. This could take an hour, two hours or an entire day. When she could, the operator would then connect the two parties. Since we were on the road, there was no way for us to do this. Oddly enough, that night my husband was able to call me directly at the hotel from Israel. We learned that only the calls made within Poland were problematic.

I pressed my parents to leave Lodz. My father wanted to continue to look for the gravesites. We tried again and then gave up. My father was not happy. He would always remember that visit as a lost opportunity because I was nervous about getting to Krakow.

Krakow

Krakow was a beautiful city that had retained some of its former elegance. We hired a driver for the day, feeling it would be a more efficient way to travel in the city. We headed to the former Jewish section of Krakow and arrived at the synagogue. The outer white wall was topped with red tiles on either side of a pitched roof. The roof sat above two enormous dark arched wood and metal double doors. Surrounding the doors was a frame whose arch was engraved with Hebrew writing. It said Beit Haknesset Chadash ReshMemAleph ZionTadekAleph (the name of the synagogue—The New Synagogue—with the initials in Hebrew of someone, followed by the initials meaning "May the memory of the righteous be a blessing"). Beyond the doors was a courtyard, behind which was the synagogue and, to its right, a cemetery. The synagogue was closed to the public when we were there, but the cemetery was open. The cemetery was small and the tombstones, inscribed in Hebrew, were old and worn. Along one of the walls of the cemetery stood pieces of headstones of varying sizes and conditions. Gravestone fragments were scattered in the cemetery. We talked to a Jewish man who still lived in Krakow. He told us that the Germans ripped out the gravestones and used them to pave the roads. When the war ended, the Jews who remained retrieved the stones and returned them to the cemetery. My dad continued to talk with him as my mom and I walked back into the courtyard. An elderly Polish Catholic woman sat on a chair behind a table. She said she was employed by the city as caretaker of the synagogue. She and my mother began talking. She told my mother that she received social security but complained that it was barely enough to live on. She then accused the Jews, who had remained in Poland instead of immigrating to Israel, of staying only so that they could collect social security. After she stopped complaining, and to my utter astonishment, my mother opened up her wallet and gave the woman money! I was disgusted with this woman's overt anti-Semitism. This Polish woman had no qualms about maligning Jews. I asked my mother why on earth she had given the woman money. My mother waved her hand and said something like she was old and poor. To this day I am baffled as to what motivated my mother to do something like that.

Our next visit was to the location of Płaszów, the concentration camp that *Schindler's List* later made famous. What had been the site of the ghetto was an open field that retained no remnant of its notorious past. Where once grass had been trampled into mud and dirt by thousands of imprisoned Jews, green grass waved in the breeze and trees stood tall. A small granite memorial to the Jews of the ghetto stood in the open field. Not far away stood an enormous memorial honoring the Polish victims of the war. The memorial depicted five heads bowed at 90-degree angles above bodies with six arms across. At the shoulder level of the two central figures was space through which one could see the sky. Cows grazed nearby. A woman and young boy, with their bikes nearby, were talking. I could not help noticing scratches into the memorial. In large capital letters at eye level, was "Jude," the German word for "Jew."

We visited the Wawel Castle on the Vistula River. It is large and imposing. It dates back to Casimir III the Great, who reigned from 1333 to 1370. I was bewildered when I saw Poles crawling on their hands and knees up the stairs to the entrance and then through the entrance. My mother said that the tombs of saints were inside. I do not remember much else about my visit to the Wawel.

Auschwitz

Auschwitz is about a 40-minute drive from Krakow, in the Polish city of Oswiecim. As we drove along the green-forested roads, I tried to imagine what it was like for the Jews during WWII. I saw partisans hiding in the woods. I saw parents moving desperately with their children, hoping to be invisible. I saw Jews in rags trying to stay warm. I saw the urgency of trying to find food in the winter when there is barely anything to eat. I saw the skinny figures wrapped in thin, frayed blankets. No fires, to heat one's frozen limbs, because they would be signals to the enemy that someone was there. I saw the train, with the tens of cattle cars pulling Jews stuffed into them. I saw my father. I saw my uncle Leo. I saw my faceless aunts, uncles, grandparents and cousin. I saw the train puffing smoke with German urgency to bring the Jews to their place of death. I felt myself starting to tear up. I didn't want to cry so I stopped thinking. How is it that such a beautiful summer landscape is actually an unmarked graveyard? I felt the presence of the dead in the ground. This country is one enormous cemetery.

We parked our car and made our way through the infamous wrought iron gate proclaiming that work brings freedom, "Arbeit mach frei." What master liars those Germans were. We walked under its arch along with many other people. Auschwitz was crowded. Many of the visitors were school children. My parents and I went into the building to pay the entry fee. We saw that guides were available. We hired a Polish-speaking guide because the English-speaking guides were busy with other groups. As we entered the camp, I looked around. I saw the once electrified barbed wire.

Anybody, a prisoner that touched it would get electrocuted. Before you got to it they would shoot 'em anyway. Besides this they had those guard posts, see. They would have had men there with machine guns.

The guard tower stood on grass next to a large one-story building with a pitched roof. On the side facing me were three huge doors that look like doors at a loading dock. Above the doors were three windows that one might see fronting a hayloft of a barn. There were two rows of barbed wire fencing separated by four feet of gravel. Kind of like a path. Did the Nazi guards walk along this path? Inside the electrified fence were row upon row of long one-story barrack-like structures. At one end of the area were two story structures. Again, nature mollified the harsh surroundings with its greenery. I remembered my aunt telling me that not a blade of grass could grow in Auschwitz. There were too many feet trampling the ground, smothering the life out of any blade that dared to attempt to grow. She said that there were no plants, so there were no butterflies, bees or other insects that depended upon nature's beauty. There were no rats, mice or other creatures because there was no food. There were plenty of lice, though, to feed off of the filthy and cramped bodies stuffed into the camp.

We walked on to a section of the camp that is populated with long two-story brick buildings with windows on both floors running the entire length. Our guide told us that 300 Jews were used to build the second floors of what were originally one-story barracks. The bricks came from the houses of neighboring villages that the Germans destroyed. It all looked neat and tidy. My dad did not recognize this place. There were no brick buildings in the Auschwitz he was in. The guide explained that the brick buildings housed Christian prisoners of war, not Jews. We walked past groups of tourists and Polish school children entering and exiting buildings. Each building told a different story of the horrors at Auschwitz. We entered a building. Photographs of piles of Jewish belongings lined the walls. On another building was a placard telling about an uprising in Auschwitz. In 1944, Jews, with the intent of breaking out, staged an uprising. They were unsuccessful and were executed. We entered another building. Inside stood a granite memorial with the inscription 1940-1945. Atop the structure was an urn containing human ashes. A floor-to-ceiling stone wall stood nearby, inscribed in different languages that say:

The people were selected on the railway platform those to be
Gassed were assured that they were going to take a bath.
Dummy showers were fixed to the ceiling. Cudgelled and

Hallooed with dogs 2000 victims were crammed in the cham
Ber 200 square meters/approx. 235 sq. yards/ in area
The chamber door was locked and Cyclon B was poured
After 15-20 minutes, the chamber was opened. Corpses
Were stripped of gold teeth, hair, earring, rings and then
Transported to a crematory. Victims personal documents
Were destroyed.

I thought of my grandmother, Aunt Haya and her five-year-old son Yossel. Nearby, a miniature replica of the crematorium showed guards aiming their rifles at the Jews. Below were miniature people packed into the gas chamber. I followed the miniature replica to my right. Piles of bodies awaited cremation. The Jews of the Sonndercomando transferred the bodies to the ovens.

My parents listened and talked to the guide as I videoed. I surprised myself. I was in Auschwitz and was stalwart. I had not broken down as I had expected I might in this place of horrors.

We entered a building that housed piles of tin cans and cloth behind glass. Next to the cloth enclosure I saw a sign.

Haircloth Made of Human Hair
Macroscopic, microscopic and micrometric
Examination of the two hair formations
Taken from two pieces of haircloth proves
That it is human hair. Most probably woman's
Hair.

The cloth looked like bolts of cloth one might see at a fabric store. Nothing out of the ordinary was visible. Thrown into another glass enclosure were brushes: hairbrushes, toothbrushes, bathing brushes, shoe brushes, shaving brushes. Anything with bristles. In another glass case there were the shoes. Piles upon piles of shoes ran nearly the length of the barrack. The barrack was full of layers of shoes, thrown in helter-skelter on both sides of the hallway. Shoes in every imaginable position: sole up, sole down, upright on heel, upright on toe. Thousands upon thousands of women's and men's shoes. Then there was the room with suitcases. Names on suitcases: Schwartz, Levy, Rubin, Weiss. Some had destinations written on them: Warsaw, Berlin, Lodz. None had the destination marked Hell. So unsuspecting were the innocent Jews. An enclosure filled with woven baskets. Neatly laid out behind glass were children's clothes.

Little shoes, little shirts, little jackets. When the Nazis rounded up Jews, they told them to bring dishes, pots, pans and kitchen utensils for their new homes. Thousands of different utensils sat behind glass in Auschwitz. Small round cans of shoe polish in another case. The Nazis determined that people with infirmities had no place in the Aryan nation. The piles of crutches and prostheses tells the story of what happened to those who were not perfect. The Germans saved the prostheses for German soldiers who returned imperfect from their war. More artifacts. Rows of tallit hanging on clotheslines. A glass case containing eyeglasses, frames looking up, down, sideways with their metal arms twisted around one another, entangled like piles of corpses in mass graves. There is so much behind glass. It is hard to fathom.

Another inscription in five different languages:

During the camps existence 405,222 prisoners-men,
Women and children-were introduced on the records.
From this number about 340,00 persons perished in
Auschwitz and other concentration camps.

This number is too low. Over one million died at the hands of the Nazis in Auschwitz.

Nailed to the wall, again behind glass, were striped shirts, pants, coats and a cap. A couple of shirts and a jacket were not striped. Wooden clogs that looked like Dutch shoes with pointed toes curving up, backless sandals and a pair of ankle height boots sat below the striped clothing. The skeletal conditions of the women found in Auschwitz, with their abnormally large knees in proportion to the size of their stick-thin legs, were displayed in heartbreaking photographs. On the other side of the photographs was another memorial. This one was a sculpture of emaciated women sitting pitifully on the ground. Each woman held a ragged cloth over her head. HUNGER was its title. There were pictures of children in striped uniforms. Below them were the clothes of the youth imprisoned there. Mengele's imprisoned children. Children unworthy of life, sub-humans, to be used and abused for medical experiment purposes. Mengele the Angel of Death.

Prisoners of war were not considered to be subhuman, so they were treated moderately better than the Jews were at Auschwitz. Depicted in one of the barracks were their living conditions. They did not have to sleep on concrete, dirt or wooden planks. Rather, they had hay mattresses. The lucky ones had mattresses of hay stuffed into sacks. They had flushing toilet facilities, albeit rows of toilets with no privacy walls. The POWs could wash in long sink-like troughs. The person in charge of the barrack had his own room with a bed, on which were a mattress and linens. He had a table and dishes.

We walked to the crematorium building. Inside were large brick ovens. Leading to each oven were metal tracks upon which the prisoners pushed wagons filled with the corpses that had been gassed. A large room next to the crematorium was the "shower" facility where gassing took place.

We left the crematorium and entered another building. My father talked to our guide as my mother and I moved into another room. I stood in front of a small glass enclosure in which there was a pile of something that I could not identify. My mother read the description as I videoed. The case contained human hair. Suddenly I felt sick. Nausea welled up in me. I started breathing hard. I turned off the camera and told my mother that I was going to throw up. I was going to throw up on the shiny clean tile floor in front of the case with human hair. My mother told me that I cannot throw up here, now, in this room. I swallowed. I breathed. I burst into uncontrollable sobs. I was sobbing and shaking and I could not stop. My mother told me it was okay and to stop crying. My father and our guide came into the room and looked at me. Now they were uncertain about whether I could continue the tour. I had to get control of myself. I breathed deeply and got a grip.

Our next visit was to the prison-within-the prison. I had never heard of a prison containing a prison. What kind of mind thinks of putting a prison inside of a prison? Our guide pointed out the standing torture chamber. Each cell was narrow enough to fit a standing human who had no possibility of changing his position; it was impossible to kneel or sit in the enclosure. Prisoners were left there for days at a time without food or water. The firing squad of the prison within the prison had its own shooting gallery. Prisoners' blood stained the wall and floor. We saw the facility where Mengele carried out his cruel experiments on Jews. How does one absorb so much inhumanity and brutality? Is barbarity on such a grand scale too much for the normal mind to grasp?

The guide asked us if we would like to see the Jewish barrack. I was perplexed. What was a Jewish barrack in this place that murdered over one million Jews? We walked past rows and rows of barracks that changed from brick to wood. There were no visitors in this area. This was strange. Our guide knocked on a door. We waited. She knocked again. Someone opened the door. Our guide talked to her and then motioned for us to come. As we entered, the lights went on.

Surrounding us were hundreds of photographs of European Jewry now vanished. A vibrant culture that had suffered through anti-Semitic laws, pogroms and in five years, annihilated by the Germans. Gone. Melancholic Yiddish music entered this somber room. I was overcome by the sadness of it all. I looked around me at the floor to ceiling haunting photographs of children, teenagers, mothers, fathers, grandparents, Jews in black, Jews in modern clothing, old, young, working, studying, some candid, others posed. They stared back at me. Jewish people slaughtered because of senseless anti-Semitism, false notions of superiority, lies, and the willingness of good people to look away and ignore the calamity occurring before them. The photographs and music were more than I could bear. I was about to break down again. I rushed out of the barracks. I breathed deeply. My parents and the guide came outside and asked me if I was okay. I said yes, but I really was not. I was overcome with despair. Being in Poland overwhelmed me.

We left Auschwitz and drove a mile to Birkenau. My father recognized where he arrived on August 28, 1944. He recognized the long brick building with the tall tower at its center, the train tracks that transported the Jews to the inferno. The entrance to the tower had a huge opening above which were two small windows. The windows looked like little eyes sitting above the opening—an enormous mouth that would swallow anyone who passed through.

The train came to this gate into this camp.

We walked into the large tower and up the stairs to the glass lookout. Spread out before us was acre upon acre of green field surround by the once electrified fence. About 20 long, one-story wooden barracks remained.

This was the men's section. See, look at all the barracks they burned down. See they remained, those posts. See over there? Those were all barracks.

We walked into one of the wooden barracks. On each side were three tiered wooden bunks running the entire length of the barrack. They looked to be about seven feet deep. There was also a brick oven with a chimney running up to the roof. My father told us that there were no bunks nor a stove where he was. In the barrack where he was, the men slept on the concrete floor. The next barrack we entered had no bunks. It had a cement floor, with wood posts anchored in it that reached up to the roof. This barrack was defined by the three long rows of cement about two-and-a-half feet wide and two feet high. Each cement row had a top containing two rows of holes running the entire length of the center of the barrack. This was the toilet facility.

I noticed the wooden guard tower surrounding the camp. I also noticed the wildflowers growing. The prisoners would have eaten them. But never mind; life did not flourish then in Auschwitz/Birkenau. This was a death camp. The guide told us that the place where the crematoria stood was at the other end of the camp. We declined to walk there. I regret that now.

Back at the tower before we left Birkenau, we met a survivor and her son who were visiting from Canada. The son was about my age. After a few minutes of conversation, we left Auschwitz and began our return to Warsaw.

We passed many villages along the way to Warsaw. I was curious about what a shtetl looked like. I stopped the car when my parents saw a community that looked like a typical shtetl. I looked at the houses from the rear, the side facing the road. The bungalow style houses were made of wood with pitched roofs. They were surrounded by weather worn gray picket fences about five feet tall. The grass in the yards was uncut. Behind one house I saw what appeared to be a small vegetable garden. A man on a wagon, pulled by a white horse, pulled up to the side of the house. He stood in the wagon and with his pitchfork he heaved his wagonload of hay into the attic of the house. I looked to my left and spotted three brown chickens pecking around in the grass next to the main road. We drove a bit farther and I saw a woman leading one cow down the road. We saw a farmer plowing his fields with an ox on a yoke.

Visit to Warsaw

We returned to the Holiday Inn in Warsaw. Coincidentally, we met again the Canadian mother and her son. They too were staying at the hotel.

At this point in our trip, there was nothing I would have rather done than leave this country. However, we had a couple of days left to sightsee before our flight to Israel.

The next day, we hired a driver to take us around. We visited the only synagogue left standing in Warsaw. Instead of destroying it, the Germans converted it to horse stalls. The Jews who remained in Warsaw after the war cleaned it up and returned it to its prewar beauty. White and beige rococo patterns topped the columns surrounding the dark wooden pews on the lower level. Arches connected ornate white columns, surrounding the sanctuary. The windows were set deeply within framed arches. The balcony façade was adorned with side-by-side embellished circles above leaf motifs. The arc on the bimah (the stage) was surrounded by dark brown marble columns. The whole effect was stunning. We spoke with one of the members of the synagogue. He said that only elderly Jews over the age of 70 were left in the city. He said that no bar mitzvahs or weddings had been celebrated in the synagogue since the war. The young Jews had left Poland for America and Europe.

Our next destination, the memorial to the Jews of the Warsaw Ghetto and the Jewish resistance fighters of the Warsaw Ghetto uprising, was erected in the area where the ghetto once stood. The memorial was in an open green park-like area. There was a large metal sculpture embedded in a stone wall at one end of the grassy area. The sculpture was in relief. On the sidewalk, about 500 feet from the memorial wall, someone had placed a three-sided Styrofoam board with pictures of Jews being tormented by the Nazis. On the ground, in front of the board, were two WWII German helmets and one Russian helmet. Why the Russian helmet, I asked my father? He had no idea. There was a stone memorial to the ghetto and the uprising. My father translated what is inscribed in Polish into English:

From the 19th of April to the 15th of May, 1943
The uprising happened in the ghetto of Warsaw
The heroic battle by the Jewish fighters
The honor of human beings

There was another granite stone inscribed at the site of the bunker of the Jewish Fighting Organization, ZOB. It detailed the German intent to find the individuals leading the uprising and their bunker. Here, the Germans surrounded the bunker and began a full-scale attack. Gas bombs were thrown into the bunker, at which time the Jewish fighters decided to commit suicide. After shooting his mother, Miriam, the first to commit suicide was Lejb Rothblat. Mordechai Anielewicz and his girlfriend, Mira Fuchrer, killed themselves. A few fighters managed to find a new escape exit. Among those who escaped were Michael Rosenblat and Prosha Altman. They joined the partisans but were later killed.

Sitting on a bench nearby was an elderly man. As we approached, he began to talk with us in Yiddish. After the war, he had chosen to remain in Poland. Later, my parents told me that there were a couple of reasons why a Jew would have selected to stay. One reason might be that the Jew married a Catholic Polish woman after the war. Another reason could be that he was a Communist and, for ideological reasons, opted to stay in Poland.

Our next stop was Umschlagplatz, the section of Warsaw that the Germans used to herd Jews for shipment to their deaths. There were groups of Jewish young people nearby. I saw a young man wearing a t-shirt with a big Jewish star on the back of it.

From this place, they shipped out to the crematorium, 300,000 Jews from this place. Here was the holding pen. From here they came and took'em to the extermination camp.

The monument was composed of marble tile walls about eight feet tall. At its center was an empty area with black tiles on the ground. There were two tiles with inscriptions, one in Hebrew and the other in English:

ALONG THIS PATH
OF SUFFERING
AND DEATH
OVER 300,000 JEWS
WERE DRIVEN IN 1942-1943
FROM THE WARSAW GHETTO
TO THE GAS CHAMBERS
OF THE NAZI
EXTERMINATION CAMPS

We visited the attractively restored Old Town. The quaint narrow and colorful buildings, surrounding a large plaza, were three and four stories high. They were a sharp contrast to the rest of Warsaw. The King's pink palace along the plaza had also been restored. The driver took us to Lazienki Palace, a baroque palace located in Warsaw's Royal Baths Park. The path leading to the palace was bordered by unattended overgrown green lushness. The palace was white and worn looking. It stood in what had once been an exclusive and wealthy area of Warsaw.

Leaving Mom and me to follow, my father walked ahead talking with the taxi driver. They looked like old friends walking and talking. Like my mother's gift of money to the anti-Semitic synagogue caretaker in Krakow, my father's affability with the driver confused me. When I asked my dad about my observation, he said he was just talking with him. Yet I could help wondering: What was going on? Sometimes I wonder if just being back in Poland felt like home. Perhaps it was speaking their mother tongue in the country where they began their lives. I have never been able to come up with an answer.

The next day, before our flight to Israel, we walked past empty stores through the depressing streets of Warsaw. On the front of one building was written in large letters, "Polska dla Polakow." "Poland for the Poles." Across the side of another building, written in Polish in large letters was, "Precz z żydowską rządem." "Down with the Jewish Government." My parents chuckled. They commented that this is the same anti-Semitic place they knew and it would never change.

Our next destination, walking distance from the hotel, was Mila 18, the location of the resistance in the Warsaw ghetto and where the only remaining wall of the Warsaw ghetto still stands. It was no easy task finding this remnant of a wall. There were no signs, only the name of the street. Mila 18 is tucked away in a courtyard at the rear of a brick building, making it difficult to find. The only reason this remnant of the ghetto was still standing was because it was the rear outside wall of the building whose front was on the inside of the ghetto.

The night before our departure for Israel, as our parents conversed, the Canadian man and I exchanged thoughts about our trips. We agreed that our visit to Poland had been extremely unpleasant. We could not shake the feeling that wherever we went, we were in one big Jewish cemetery. So depressing. During this conversation, it became clear that our decision to rent a car was fortunate. The Canadian and his mother had hired a driver for their weeklong trip. He told me that the driver's car had broken down on a side road on either the first or second day out. I do not remember the details of their unpleasant experience, but I do remember that he said that he wished they had rented a car.

The next morning, we returned to the dilapidated airport and boarded our El Al flight to Israel. Never have I been happier to leave a country. I looked out the window as the plane pulled away from the terminal. I saw military vehicles surrounding the airplane and following us to the take-off strip. The plane took off. I breathed a sigh of relief and slept all the way to Israel.

Conclusion

The magnitude of the sufferings and losses of the Holocaust victims are beyond comprehension. My parents' stories, as horrific as they are, are two in millions. Every European Jew had his or her own horrendous experiences, most of which we will never hear or read about. The loss of Jewish lives and their potential contributions to life on Earth will never be known. The theft and destruction of Jewish properties reaches into the billions and their true value will never be recompensed. Survivors knew all of this to be true. The one satisfaction left for them was that, because they lived, they won. Hitler, Goring, Eichmann, Goebbels and the others in the decadent Nazi machine were unable to destroy the Jewish people. The survivors understood that, as difficult as it was, they would continue with their lives and succeed. Succeed for themselves, their post Holocaust families, their lost families and the greater Jewish community. And succeed they did. They are a generation of Jews who made castles out of ashes.

Family of Anna & Daniel Geslewitz

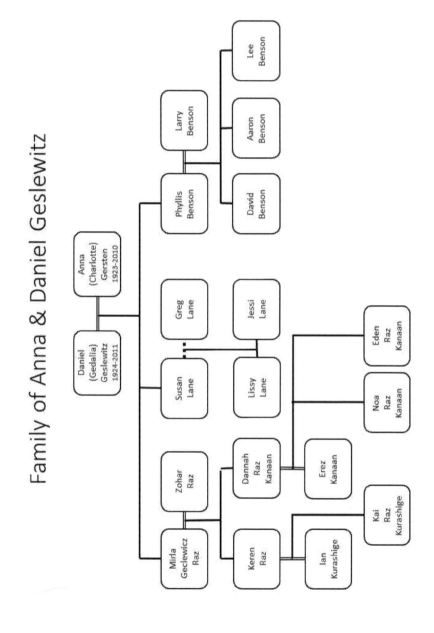

Bibliography

Bentwich, Norman. (1955-1956). International aspects of restitution and compensation for victims of the Nazis. The British Yearbook of International Law, 32, 204-217.

Burstin, Barbara. (2009). Holocaust survivors: rescue and resettlement in the United States. Jewish Women: A Comprehensive Historical Encyclopedia. Jewish Women's Archive.

Cohen, Beth. (2007). <u>Case Closed: Holocaust Survivors in Postwar America</u>. New Brunswick: Rutgers University Press

Friedman Filip (1945). Zagłada Żydów lwowskich (Extermination of the Jews of Lwów), Lodz: Centralna Zyd. komisja historyczna w Polsce.

Helmreich, William, B. (1996). <u>Against All Odds: Holocaust Survivors and the Successful Lives They Made in America</u>. New Brunswick: Transaction Publishers.

Rabinowitz, Dorothy. (1976). <u>New Lives: Survivors of the Holocaust Living in America</u>. Alfred A. Knopf, New York.

Robinson, Nehemiah. (1962). Spoliation and remedial action: the material damage suffered by Jews under persecution, reparations, restitution, and compensation. Nehemiah, Institute of Jewish Affairs World Jewish Congress.

Rosensaft, Menachem, and Rosensaft, Joana. (2001). The early history of Jewish-German reparations. Fordham International Law Journal, 25, S1-45.

Sagi, N. (1986). <u>German Reparations: A History of the Negotiations</u>. Jerusalem: The Magnes Press.

Poems by Anna Gersten Geslewitz

September 17, 1923 – December 14, 2010

The Holocaust poems are dedicated to the memory of my parents, Marcus and Sarah Gersten, my sisters, Ella and Fanny, my brother, Leon, and the six million Jews who perished during those tragic times.

Memories, memories! When you get to my age you largely live on memories. How often have I tried to rid myself of them, but the brain just stubbornly refuses. Life defenses, which bid us to forget all those tragic, apocalyptic moments, have an unending conflict with reality. Time, professed by so many to be a curing agent, continues to reflect on the past and presses deeper and deeper into my soul. Though fifty-six years have passed since those calamitous days of World War II and those disastrous times of Nazism, my soul has not shaken off the dust of sorrow and anguish. I tried to resist my deep disappointment in a world that stood idly by while Nazi crimes were being committed, unconcerned about the fate of its victims. I try to find reasons that explain why the Jews have been persecuted for so many centuries and find no acceptable justification. Jews, in most countries which they were allowed entrance, created prosperity, made considerable contributions in the fields of education, art, medicine, research, sciences, and entertainment, and had a very small crime rate.

It is well-documented that the persecution of the Jews came to fruition when Christianity became dominant in Europe and the Jews were the only ones to reject it. Through indoctrination many churches instilled in their members a belief that the Jews killed Christ and were the cause of many of the world's ills. The majority of the European Christian population accepted those falsehoods. Not until John XXIII became Pope did the Vatican Counsel partially remove these accusations and falsehoods. Perhaps the Pope's corrections relaxed the common beliefs injurious to Jews, but they still failed to eliminate anti-Semitism. Though we saw many phases of Jewish persecution in Europe, where Jews were excluded from public and governmental positions, prevented from residing among non-Jews, barred from attending higher institutions of learning, forced to suffer through many programs, and banished from countries (i.e. the Spanish Inquisition), the worst was yet to come.

Hitler's entrance into the political arena brought about the worst outbreak of anti-Semitism in Europe and beyond. The medieval accusations of the Jews being demonic, using Christian blood in their rituals, spreading the plague, etc... gave way to more sophisticated accusations of modern times: Jews being manipulative in their desire to achieve world dominance and devious in their ways of influencing the world in financial markets. Suddenly, the Jews became, depending on the country they were residing in, either communists or capitalists. In communist countries they were accused of being capitalists and in capitalist countries they were accused of having communist connections.

In Poland, Jews constituted the largest minority and it became the most fertile ground for Hitler's ideologies regarding Jews. Polish anti-Semitism was fed by the modern and medieval prejudices. The Poles' hatred toward the Jews was a result of centuries old indoctrination by religious institutions.

In the 14th century, King Casimir the Great, in order to revitalize Poland's slumping economy, invited Jews to settle there, hence Poland became the country with the largest Jewish population in Europe. Although the Jews contributed greatly to Poland's economic revitalization, the deep-seated anti-Semitism never abated.

The Ukrainians, Lithuanians, and the Germans constituted the other minorities in Poland. Ukrainians inhabited the Southeastern part and the Lithuanians mainly the Northeastern part of Poland. The Germans mainly resided in the Western part of Poland adjacent to the German border and in a few colonies not far from the Russian border. The Ukrainians and the Lithuanians, during the German invasion of Poland, were so mercilessly cruel to the Jews that the Nazis selected them as the most suitable to assist them in the destruction of the Jews.

Although before the Nazi Era all minorities lived in Poland in acceptable relations, the underlying currents of hostilities toward Jews were always seething and came to full fruition in the Nazi era. While the countries allied in the battle against Hitler were unconcerned with the fate of the Jews, in Poland the population was openly abetting the Germans in their destruction. After WWII, when it was fully discovered what atrocities were perpetrated by the Germans, the rest of the world was intensely repulsed, yet the Polish population continued their violent behavior and murdered many of the returning survivors. (Kielce, June 1946)

I was only eighteen when the Germans invaded Eastern Poland. A few months after their occupation of Lwow, we were forced to abandon our homes and enter the ghetto, which they formed on the outskirts of the city. This part of town consisted of homes and apartments with very poor and primitive facilities. But the physical depravations were not those which brought our morale to its lowest point. They were the persistent persecutions, the systematic exterminations achieved through methods never known before in history, and the hunger and dehumanization, which permeated our wretched existence. The so-called "actions," repeated raids on the ghetto population, the random shootings, the deportations to concentration camps and gas chambers, intensified my self-preservation instinct and brought about my decision to take the only survival route: to change my name and escape the Christian world as a Christian. It was the hardest decision to leave my family and enter the strange, cold world so unfamiliar to me. The poem "Remembrances" echoes those distressful feelings of pain and loneliness and the cries of helplessness:

Tear not my aching heart away
From all I have loved and lost, the day
I left to search for life elsewhere.

And then:

How do I live, survive in the wild
Away from a life with surroundings so mild?

The constant fear of being discovered made my escape as difficult as the heartbreaking separation from my family. In the poem "The Mask" I say:

Behind it I have put my true
Pale face I dared not show,
Lest my true nature gives a clue
To my ancestral flaw.

But the alternative was the death sentence, for from our ghetto the Germans constantly transported people directly to gas chambers. In the poem "The Great Crime," I described the wretched, destined to die:

There are the chimneys dark and dusty gray,
From which last hopes have fled and smoked away;
Gas chambers with hermetically closed doors,
And human ashes strewn upon the floors.

And what was left:

A throng of shadows left behind the walls
A breathless image of six million souls.

I had a powerful ally in my struggle for survival- "LIFE." I had always loved life, but my love for life was never as pronounced as in those days of being so close to losing it. I felt Life's presence on all my treacherous roads. She was my fountain of strength and she became my guardian angel. When Death pursued me and with triumphant eyes gazed at me, Life stood ready to combat him:

I felt her warming love embrace
my pining, fear torn heart
and of her fair and cloudless face
I saw myself a part.

When life seemed to be so vulnerable and survival almost impossible, our passionate love intensified. Her heart beat so close to mine, "Her soothing melodies," her bright face and balmy breath, though invisible to anyone else, were my guiding light.

Oh, how I loved her bright countenance,
Basked in her balmy breath;
She was the force in my sustenance:
Time's soul to conquer Death.

Shortly before World War II, anti-Semitism in Poland grew to alarming proportions. When the Germans entered Lwow in June of 1941, the Polish and Ukrainian population was ready and willing to assist them in disposing of the Jews. It was a few days after the occupation when the Germans gave them permission to inflict punishment on the Jews. Across from the window of our apartment was an abandoned courtyard. It was there that I observed one of countless outbursts of hate explode in the air, when an innocent young Jewish man was beaten to death. In the poem "Death in the Courtyard, "the young man:

He stood there wretched, all alone
Among the mob, a lonely stone,
A puppet with a painful frown
A circus fool, a captive clown.
The town jester masked with blood.

The tragic scene had a profound impact on my young life and never has left my memory. This was only the beginning of our tragedy. "Thorns of Remembrance" describes the sudden changes which confronted us:

We never thought the blessed grounds,
That man has trod, would bleed with wounds,
And sunshine's bright and golden ray
Would paint dead bodies with decay.

We knew we were doomed. We had no physical or moral strength to resist. The ghetto was shrinking. With every "action" more and more people were transported to camps and gas chambers.

The Germans used to gather people in the town square where they segregated them into groups. The young people were sent to labor camps, the elderly and the children were sent to death. Many were shot at random on the spot. The poem "Delirious" describes a little boy who was shot, hallucinating about his past, his town, his home, and his mother. He is saying to his mother:

168

Hold my hand, oh, help me up!
Bring the mad, mad world to stop!

How many times had I pleaded for a sign of hope, but at the end resigned myself to the thought that the heavens had abandoned us. In the poem, "Oh, Heavens Do Forgive My Wrath:"
I weep for the children from us departed,
Young lives withered in dust.

In the poem "Supplication" I cry:
Answer me! Oh, still my ire!
Ease my heart from pain so dire!

In the poem "Oh, Ease My Fear," the "eyes of my mind" still cannot find peace when I remember all the horror pictures. I still see those helpless children torn away from their mothers. I hear their piercing cries and:
Bid the world to hear
The lamenting voice of prayer's lost choice.

I plead:
Break the yoke we bear,
The deafening noise of memory's voice.

But the deafening noise could not be stilled, for I saw "The Valley of the Sorrow" filling up with "Graveyards Sown by Death." The winds were crying and carrying the voices of the doomed:
Toward the roaring rivers, gushing
Blood and tears bursting from
The grave filled, torn earth's womb

The echo of those voices returns from the:
Deaf and heedless lands,
Where the evil spirit stands,
Carries voices of tomorrow
Back to the valley of the sorrow.

The voices of those ill-fated struck the world's deaf ear.

"The Clouds of Freedom"

Those frightful years, how far away,
But, yet, they linger on today.
The torment of a broken youth,
The crumbling of a jolted truth;
The long dead ideologies
Like lofty words of eulogies,
The rupture of a peaceful world
Into a violent, eddying whirl,
The long lost voices, their dull refrain,
Still echo and decline to wane.And when I look upon the sky

And whispering winds my tears blow dry,
I wonder if the branded sign
Upon my brow has ceased to shine.
The painful sign of infamy,
The fainting cry of destiny.
The sign of hate for many an age
Of blind injustice in a rage.
The suffering of constricted souls
For ruthless man's insidious goals.

How many times have I defied
The mighty Death and have denied
The prowling eyes of dreadful Fate,
To court me at a final date.
And when the last pervasive cry
Has faintly died in the sky,
I didn't hear the reveling bells
Of freedom in the air swell.
For as my heart grew too cold to care,
No dreams were left for me to share.

My world sunk, fallen to the grave,
While bent low as oppressor's slave.
The bloodstained image of mankind,
Played tricks upon my eyes and mind.
The azure skies seemed threatening dark,
The stars devoid of shine and spark,

The sunrays could not penetrate
My heart so cold and desolate.
The simple mind of innocence,
Imprisoned in a frightful trance.

No road to trod for me was left,
Of all I've loved my heart bereft.
No guiding line to lead my way,
No place to go, no place to stay.
And yon way down the blue horizon
Stood walled, encircled like a prison –
A prison of a tortured mind,
Which could no peace and no hope find;
Accustomed to the eerie sights,
Bewildered by the freedom lights.

I prayed the stars would be my guide,
I prayed the wind or ocean tide,
Would carry my deserted soul
Back from the abysmal fall.
Though freed from devil's paradise,
Yet still in danger of demise
From forces living deep inside
My being, ready to collide
And tear apart the fiber strings,
Ere freedom hope to my soul brings.

How lucky is the fate of one,
Whose web of life was never spun
By devil's sly, insidious ways,
Traumatic nights and hellish days.
Whose eyes have never looked upon
A praying heart turned into stone,
When feverishly searching skies
For solace to despondent cries.
His trembling body's last defense
Abandoned to life's false pretense.

Oh yes, those years are long, long gone,
And I no longer trail alone

I stand in life's serenest age,
In calmest Autumn's golden page
And though the sign upon my brow
Has paled in soothing sunshine's glow,
My wounded heart cannot erase
The memory's remaining trace.
It cannot stop the dull refrain
Of voices lost to human bane.

"Children of a Tragic Game"

She spoke to me in a distant voice,
Concealing in her outward poise
Sad memories etched upon
Her mind, casting a dark, lone
Shadow of her troubled past,
Dwelling in her feeble chest.

If my heart could but endure
Time's professed long soothing cure,
But for some unknown purport
Destiny has sworn to sport
In a melancholy way,
With my pining heart's dismay.

I had a home once far away,
But Fate forbid me there to stay.
She threw my lot and let remain
With creatures I have deemed insane
And never since have I regained
My carefree spirit they disdained.

I traveled from the dark of night
Until the early morning light.
The nights-a sorrowful, sad cruise,
And days-the memory's worst truth.
I journeyed through the clouds of Time,
His virtues dead-no vice a crime.

I saw upon the Earth's plains
A gory sight of bloody stains.
In place of grass the stalks of life
Cut down by hangman's keenest knife.
The rivers carry from the leas
All bitter tears to distant seas.

Only the weeping willows, in time,
Have shaded the preposterous crime,
Pressing heavily on the sores,

Deep into decaying mores
Of a world that has allowed
With deathly veils its men to shroud.

Revenge is not what dwells inside
My oppressed heart, but lack of pride
The world has shown in fellow man,
And still persists now, as it did then,
With a perverted sense of truth,
To scour our souls with rude abuse.

I try to steal through a maze of thoughts
To find the long abandoned roads,
Where cast off love and deep compassion
Were lost to man's relentless passion.
If I shall find it, I'll bequeath
Upon the future, the long sought peace."

She knew not why she did confess
To me, a stranger, her distress.
No stranger was I, I explained,
For Fate has kept my life detained
And held my youth like hers and claim,
Branding us: Children of a tragic game.

"Death in the Courtyard"

It was a sweltering summer day
The air has strayed from breath away,
And in the sunshine's melting glow
The currents drifted in a slow,
Lethargic, gloomy, somber mood.
In contrast to the crowds that stood
In an abandoned, barren court,
Alive now with a savage sport.
There with wild passion of a mob,
The tyranny with pleasure throb
Exploded in a vengeance bliss
From years of hate and prejudice.
No eye has ever seen a group
In bondage to emotions stoop
So low, as reason's supplication voice
Was drowned in maddening. fearsome noise.
In a convulsive motion lost,
Across the air arose the most
Bloody, brutal, mocking throng
Of men and women in a song.
A hateful curse upon their lips,
A prelude to their mounted whips.
With lightening speed of a tempest's eye
The fiercest blasts began to fly
Into the center, where in shock
A man with painful blows was struck.

He was a man, as I recall,
Of posture slight and stature small.
His eyes weary, but not from age,
For he was in his life's young stage.
His pants seemed bit too long and baggy,
His beard in disarray and shaggy.
In a convulsive, panting breath,
His trembling body in distress,
He stood there wretched, all alone
Among the mob, a lonely stone;
A puppet with a painful frown,

A circus fool, a captive clown.
The town jester masked with blood,
A tragic figure in a flood
Of jeering, mocking, heartless souls-

The devil's pulse, his ghastly ghouls.
They tore the skullcap from his head,
They plucked his beard until he bled.
His body flinched, his bloodshed eyes
Were painfully turned toward the skies.
He shrank away with every whip
A prayer on his quivering lip.

O God, upon the heavens high,
Bring peace to me before I die,
For in your mercy I will rest,
Bring freedom to my pining chest.
His last words fell, void of sound,
His body thumped upon the ground.
He drew his breath for the last time,
His soul above the human crime.
A martyr in a flood of rage,
A victim of world's sorry stage.
A sudden wind with a rushing gust
Shrouded the body with earthly dust.

A mortal fear has gripped my heart,
I felt the pangs of grief, deep smart,
I knew now man was not born free
But chained to cruel destiny.
A chill lay heavy on my chest;
Is this how man is laid to rest?
His feelings, hopes, consumed behind
Moral decay of human mind?
Was this a signal to construe
This was the destiny of a Jew?

Those maddening memories my soul still crowd,
The voice of prejudice sounds clear and loud.
Man's inhumanity is still alive

And madness in our bounds still rife.

And when the clouds of time go by
And scattered lay beneath the sky
The graves of those without escape,
My eyes recall the human rape.
One lonely Jew, one lonely heart,
Six million Jews erased from the chart.

"Gone Are Those Gentle Days"

By a dusty, sandy road
Where the cricket and the toad
Lived in harmony with the rest
Of the earth inhabiting cast,
There stood a house I still can see
In my fondest memory.
There behind the bam on prickly
Vines raspberries grew thickly
And the cherries on the tree
Waited to be rendered free.
Chickens, geese, the horned goat
Roamed around the cooling moat.
There the cows in barn contentedly
Mooed and horses stood intently,
Waiting for a human form
To relieve their inner storm
To be harnessed and with lust
Cross the yard and kick the dust.
When the day from night has broken,
Nature from her slumber woken,
With crimson petals her blooms arrayed
The fragrant rose with pride displayed.

The lazy river slowly flowed
Sneaking through the riverbed, glowed
Midst the golden fields of corn
Vanishing, never to return
Its bubbling murmur in my ears
Still brings a sentimental tear.

Oh, how I love on a lonely night
To reminisce beneath the moonlight
And carry memories from those days
To follow my thoughts warmest rays.
I still see the peaceful place;
In my heart remains a space
Where the memories of each summer
Bring my mind into a calmer

State of childhood, a cheerful glee
Away from the city's rushing sea.
I still hear in the breeze of spring
Like gentle songs the voices ring
With love and happiness in the air
That birds and humans often share.
Though house and barn still humbly stand
Yet now it is a far off land.
No soul is left, no cheerful song
And gentleness forgotten long.
The river still flows endlessly
But now its waters listlessly
Repeat the faint, perplexing cry
Of haunted souls condemned to die.
Up way above the riverbed
The souls of ghosts the water tread
Taking the doom of the lost dream
Into the depth of the flowing stream.
Veiled in the misty, lingering fog,
The cricket and the croaking frog
Still live in harmony, though instead
Of living souls, caress the dead.

"Liberation"

Rejoice you captive souls, rejoice
Hark to the Liberation's fiery voice.

Triumphantly the bells of freedom rang
Gone was the hatred spewing gang
And where once deathly winds have blown,
Where filled with fear the birds have flown
From graves of men in their prime stolen,
And rivers full of tears ran swollen,
Where hate presided over love
And evil killed the peaceful dove,
Came Liberation in its glory.
Yet, freedom held a dismal story.
A rude awakening from a stream
Of shattered hopes, a ghastly dream
Of wasted lives, the henchman's hand
Still vivid on the executioner's stand.

We lost the count of days and years
The hopelessness has dried our tears.
We have endured a mass destruction
Ignored by world's detached reaction,
Were followed by a wild pursuit
Of a sadistic longing to uproot,
Disgrace, ravage and eliminate,
To mastermind our wretched fate.
And when the breath of freedom blew
And the sun its rays around us strew,
No revelry could cheer our hearts
Uprooted from familiar parts.
A captive mind does not easily adjust
To freedom's sudden, shocking thrust;
A wounded heart does not easily repair
Its painful scars wrought by despair.

Yet, time in its prophetic way
Carries a healing, comforting ray
Of hope, and each new day would shed

A part of our previous dread,
So when through crevices of a dismal thought
A brighter light its way has fought,
The voices from the mountain crest
Have summoned us to a greater test.

We knew we must regain the will
We had a destiny to fulfill.
We had to show the cowardly brutes
Our great existence came from roots
Of indestructible moral strain
Throughout a history of afflictions and pain.
We are the witnesses to darkest history
An era of strangled powers of liberty,
An era of lies, deceit, and slander
Civilizations to beastly rules surrender.

Oh, shed your guise you nations who pretend
In all your bigotry as guardians to stand.
Though ours is the torment of inexorable pain,
Yours is the scourge of an indelible stain.
We who were forced the brutes to obey
A moral of import have now to convey:
To foe and friend a message to carry
That living evidence they could not bury.

"Hitler"

He's dead! And with him buried is the lust
Of power, that turned honor into dust;
Had carried shouts of a perverted tongue,
Chained our freedom and bells of death had rung.
He's dead! His breath will never more exude
The poison his accursed mouth had spewed.
The lethal breath of death.

Oh, heavens! All the ghastly sites he drew,
With the help of his own devil's crew.
A master drawing of deception,
Of shocking horror-rendition of a demented mind's collection.
A picture of the vanishing shadows,
Departing from life's haunting meadows.
A sight of ghastly death.

Repent, oh, Nature, for your most vile crime!
For breathing life into a monster of all times;
Repent for peace you gave him when he lost his breath,
For, what he earned, is a many, many millions death.
Repent for the earth he to convulsions shook,
Tormented souls he to the graveyards took.
Repent, oh, Nature!

And what price Glory did your fancy pay,
For the rapture of a sick mind with a posture of clay?
A garden of souls broken, torn,
Unsung elegies and a pile of stones spread over the forlorn,
Wretched bodies sacrificed to a maligned hero,
As Rome has burned to delight the eyes of Nero.
What price, Glory!

And you, Humanity, have looked upon the wretched,
When from his height he wielded his deft hatchet.
Perhaps your wings of mercy were beyond
The reach of man's compassion — that holds the human bond.
Or were they pulled by strings attached to people's minds,
Whenever they would wind emotions, or unwind?
What sorry thought, Humanity!

All those, who so revered him dearly,
And as divine perceived him nearly,
What heritage has his name left?
Just lonely graves and minds of dignity and human worth bereft.
A legacy of terror, tyranny, and gross disaster,
To those who helped him rise and made him to be master.
A torturing legacy of death.

"I Dare Not Dream"

I dare not dream of youthful passions,
Of starry nights in lovely sessions,
The warming sun, the fragrant air,
I dare not dream of morning fair.

I dare not dream of high above
Where sky and clouds combine in love,
Where birds, their pinions stretched, are free,
I dare not dream, I dare not be.

I dare not dream of drifting air
To bring good rides with me to share.
I gaze into the dark abyss
And dare not dream life's wondrous bliss.

I dare not dream of music flowing
Through breezes of the wind come blowing
To whisper on my window sill.
I dare not dream, my yearnings fill.

I dare not dream of life out there,
Proud nature and the muses share.
My thoughts run in forbidden stream.
I dare not dream, I dare not dream.

"The Wandering Soul"

I once saw a soul wandering around
Deserted, desolate graves,
Her tears swallowed by the withered ground
Below the whirlwind's waves.

How I remember happy times
Within warm beating hearts,
Where youth with love together rhymes
Their life's delights and smarts.

One day the tempest shook my slumber
The still of night has broke,
The dreadful noise like falling timber
The earth with tremor rocked.

The tyrant's treacherous resources,
Abysmal Nature's fall,
The shocks of heaven's stormy forces
Have silenced sorrow's call.

My muted voice with anguish moans
But cannot reach the depth
Where widely scattered lie the bones
And Nature above weeps.

There is no place for me to dwell,
I wearily steal through thorns
To reach the tombs where bodies fell
And chain of Death adorns.

I live secluded now, apart,
The empty stone my bed,
Wounded by poisoned, bloodstained dart,
A phantom of the dead.

A phantom roaming amid the stars
Beneath the cold-faced moon,
And in the depth of seas, afar
From spheres of gentle tunes.

I sweep the air, I tread the earth,
Invisible to mortals, I walk behind a mourner's hearse

Then glide through heaven's portals.

The soul rose and with a sigh
Fled the lifeless stone,
With guiding stars approaching sky
His lonely form has shone.

"The Chosen Children of the Chosen People"

They were born at sunrise
They expired at sundown
The chosen children
Of the chosen people.
They were thrown to the dragon
His fire consumed them
And spit out smoke and ashes
From chimneys gray.
The choking souls
Wrapped in innocence
In mist enveloped
Into evanescence fled.
The sunshine burnt
The moonlight chilled,
In darkness lost
The heavens stood unmoved.
The weeping willow
Broke laden with tears,
The wind has fled
Laden with sin.
The morning mist
Enshrouded the crime;
The devil sang
His joyful song,
Mercy departed
Drawn by the beast
From shadow's path
Into a mute world.

"Mother"

The night is dark, the stars are gone
And I must ponder all alone.
My loved ones gone, no one to share
The gripping pain I cannot bear,
I see the gentle face that bore
The smile now silent tears adorn.
The tears deep frozen to her cheek,
And lips too cold again to speak.
They were alive once when he came,
Took her away her life to claim.
He called on Death to fill his score,
The burning fever he had for
Unsightly, agonizing plays
To boost his ego's triumph days.
He was the court, the judge and jury,
The voice of persecution fury.
Your crime mother-undesirable race,
The sentence-death without a sign or trace.

Oh, mother, love will never crown
His cold eyes, for his soul will drown
In tyranny of lost emotions.
An abject slave to wrong devotions.
A craven man, he did not know
He has slain sunray's brightest glow.
For in your simple love was dressed
A mother's glory unsurpassed

Though in a place you dwell unknown,
There nature's flowers will be sown
Of love, behind a veil of sorrow
Concealed in hopes for better morrow.
And when from oceans shall rebound
The echoes of a gentle sound,
The voice that calms the storming shore
Will carry me to days of yore.
I shall behold your lovely face
Forever in the lonely place,

Where memories are searching for
The brighter hues of human lore.
And when the rose I blooming see
Bedewed with tears, my thoughts will flee
To the distant place where I have left,
Of you my aching heart bereft.

"Thorns of Remembrance"

I
Eighteen years of age was I
When all of us were doomed to die;
We broke the law that every man
Of the same crime be guilty can.
Our right to life had no excuse,
For we were born to the creed of Jews.

Three girls were we and the youngest boy,
We loved him like a precious toy;
Abounding curls upon his head,
Angelic face in sunshine clad.
In those early days but no one knew,
What bitter fate awaits the Jew.

We never thought that nature's palm,
So soft now, so serene and calm,
Would turn into a stony fist
And fling our lives into dark mist.
That torrents of wild hatred grew,
And mortal tides approached the Jew.

We never thought the blessed grounds,
That man has trod, would bleed with wounds;
And sunshine's bright and golden ray
Would paint dead bodies with decay.
We didn't know how close time grew,
When men will strike the helpless Jew.

II
My brother now only seventeen,
Was tall and fair, his body lean,
His eyes like skies, dark azure blue,
Reflected all that's good and true.
The German who my brother slew,
Thought him to fair to be a Jew.

The skies have paled (they told me so),
The raging winds lamented woe,
Sun rays through clouds winding, spired,
Shrouded the body where life expired.
Swallows mute upon the bough,
Palsied watched the crime below.
He was the youngest of us all,
Yet, death came first on him to call.
Oh, how my heart for him had pined,
It broke my soul, it writhed my mind.
I loathed that foe, his poisoned dart,
That killed my brother and chained my heart.

III
Suffering tends to build a wall,
After disasters take their toll;
A wall of strength and moral force,
To aid you on your tottering course.
I bore the strength one only has,
Whose heart has heard the voice of death.

Now I was the youngest of us three,
But by some measure of degree,
My zest for life, my fear to die,
Led all my senses to defy
The foe, who in a torturing way
Stood ready to attack the prey.

I felt my passions rise and grow,
I saw the light of hope still glow;
A beam of light that stayed with me
On my blind road toward destiny.
I had to run, run for my life,
Hence to escape their jagged knife.

I ran, I ran, and didn't look,
When horrors earth and heaven shook,
I panicked when I heard the calls
Of trembling shadows on the walls;
A kind of agonizing fear,
When panic at your senses tear.

For when I threw a backward glance,
I saw the devils laugh and dance;
My mind pursued by the voice of doom,
Resounding from the earth's womb,
Turned silence into piercing scream —
A nightmare, mortifying dream.

IV
My older sister shared with me,
My rocky road that destiny
Prepared for us in a time,
When the ferocity of crime
Was raging over war torn plains
And clanged the sorry song of chains.

My parents then were still alive,
Their lives but had no strength to strive,
In a hole they hid beneath the floor,
The place they learned to abhor.
No air to breathe and void of light
A cursed dungeon would seem bright.

Until betrayed they were brought to die;
Now in an unknown grave they lie —
Torn from the roaring, maddening screams,
Injustice echoed in endless streams
Of vanished young and old alike,
When man came other man to strike.

V
Sixty-three years upon me lie
With memories that refuse to die;
The memories of my tender years
Passed away in grief and tears;
When faith in man was lost forever,
In violence and madness fever.

Madness, which for long decried
Man, who had ferociously defied
Basic human rights which nature

Gave to every living creature.
Men who with contempt and scorn,
Brought this earth to weep and mourn.

"The Voice of Prejudice"

Are birds in song upon a tree
Still mocking me, still mocking me?
Or pity is it they relay
For my dismay, for my dismay?
I need not pity nor derision
The world around me needs revision
To shake its prejudice.

I stand in greatness and in grace
Of Nature's gently moving pace,
Yet, forces all around me flash
Bright lights of hatred and I dash
To hide my face to blind my eyes,
To close my ears to savage lies,
The voice of prejudice.

A sea of thought upon me thrust
Is swaying my steady, stable ballast;
My judgment of humanity
From love to culpability,
While muted voices lost beneath
The stone of everlasting peace
Tell tales of prejudice.

They tell of being captive once,
Of skillful hands with fiery guns,
Of piteous sights of hatred alive,
Humanity's last breath in strife
To save the remnants of compassion
From wild pursuit and vile expression
Of rampant prejudice.

How through the age as dark as night,
The executioner's iron might,
Like deathly breath of poisoned air,
With lightening speed strewed dread and fear;
Brought maximal profanity
Back from fierce eternity
Of endless prejudice.

How the earth trembled, brave men fell,
The Passions rang the deadly knell.
The pulse of terror with rapacity,
With strength of wild ferocity,
In endless streams of fallacies
Praised in despairing melodies
The work of prejudice.

Don't sing, you birds upon a tree,
Songs that cannot set me free;
But wake the mom with last farewell
To minds imprisoned in a cell
Of bigotry, then look afar
To see descending from a star
Black death of prejudice.

"The Valley of the Sorrow"

Where the bones lay scattered now
Where the birds are preying low
And the current of the river
Chills your spine and makes you shiver,
And the never ending nightmare
Drowns your soul in cold despair,
And your heart in painful sorrow
Sees no pride in better morrow,
Those are places where behind
Tear filled waters you will find
Memories of lost desires,
Worlds consumed by burning fires.

Cornered in a traitor's glories,
In tempestuous, raging stories
Of mad, ghastly, vast proportions,
In a chain of gross distortions,
Beaten by the pulse of time,
Cast off in their early prime,
Mute and sightless to mankind,
Lost to darkness of man's mind,
Lays the world's unknown path
To the graveyards sown by Death.

There they perished and retired,
By their lawless masters mired;
Thrown by winds of crime and peril
Into fragments sank in sterile,
Hostile earth and hurled stones,
Freed from being Devil's pawns.
Now delivered to the earth
Like a loud, tumultuous curse,
With a grating, harsh derision;
Victims of a twisted vision,
Evil minds in darkness clad
By the doom dark ages bred.

And the echoes from the top
Of the mountain ranges drop
Into the valleys from the past
All the doom of those who rest
In the shadow of destruction
Decimated into fractions.
And the echo carries clamor,
Lifts the voices while the tremor
From beneath the earth and upwards,
To the heavens and back downwards
Spreads across the wide, vast barriers,
To the ghastly tidings carriers,
Bounces off the closed, deaf ears,
With a woe and anguish tears
Through the darkness of tomorrow
Back to the valley of the sorrow

Hark, oh, hark, the winds are crying
Through the branches and the flying
Birds of prey in circles wide
In a piercing voice deride
Howling wind's descending tale
Of a rising Spirit, pale,
Shaky, trembling, just returning
From a hatred torn, burning,
Yet, as cold as a winter freeze,
Passioned with a poisoned breeze,
World beyond the river current
With a wild untamable torrent.
And the winds are howling, rushing
Toward the roaring rivers, gushing
Blood and tears bursting from
The grave filled, torn earth's womb.

And the wailing wind's refrain
Silenced by the voice of bane,
Transformed into a whispering breath
By the gruesome face of Death,
In the darkness of the night
Meets the echo back from flight

Into deaf and heedless lands
Where the evil Spirit stands,
Carries voices of tomorrow
Back to the valley of the sorrow.

Cry, oh, cry, lament their lives
Lost in cumbrous, fruitless strifes,
Their voices from the dark of ages
Written into screaming pages,
Tearing through the lifeless planes.
Flowing through the bloodless veins,
Through the mountains, through the seas,
Rippling rills around the leas.
Cry for sunshine's broken ray
Lost forever, swept away
From the shadows of tomorrow
In the valley of the sorrow.

"I Had a Love Affair with Life"

I had a love affair with Life
While tramping through her thorns,
While stumbling over stretches rife
With grief of anguish born.
With chocking spasms has heaved the earth
While Life stood by me close,
When others perished in a dearth
Our passionate love arose.

When hell spewed fire all around,
And Death with burning breath,
With joy in a victorious sound,
Leaped forward with a wrath,
His eyes a crazed, beguiling smile,
Have failed to notice, that
In center of his deadly pile,
Life and my heart have met.

When dew has turned into drops of blood,
And leas with tears abound,
Have broken into a roaring flood,
A weeping, maddening sound,
In place of a merry joyous song
The birds sang eulogies,
I heard the heartbeat in a throng
Of Life's soothing melodies.

I was so young and so forlorn
Weary with cares and fear;
Why was my being so early torn
And Death came close, so near?
My heart grew faint, so heavy leaden,
My soul a captive shadow,
When from a distance my fair maiden-
Life-crossed the swollen meadow.

She crossed the meadow in one sweep
Like a billow on the sea,

For she beheld my silent weep
Heard my despairing plea.

I felt her warming love embrace
My pining, fear torn heart,
And of her fair and cloudless face
I saw myself a part.

I've drawn my strength from her fountain depth.
Have triumphed in her power,
When in those times of brute relapse
Black Death brought me to cower.
I have delighted in her voice,
Followed her airy wings,
Those times of clamoring, endless noise
Drowned in her vital springs.

Oh, how I loved her bright countenance,
Basked in her balmy breath;
She was the force in my sustenance,
Time's soul to conquer Death.
I saw her in the fragrant rose
Awakened from her sleep,
And when the lily pad arose
To eye the world from deep.

I heard her songs in the bubbling spring
In harmony with the lark,
I saw her from the rainbow bring
Bright hues to light the dark.
She kissed the flowers from the seeds,
Winged birds from lofty nests,
Her tresses throughout grassy meads
Woke Nature from her rest.

Now Time, the never-ending stream
Flows but in one direction,
Leaving the passion of my dream
Behind to my reflection.
Though may the universal law

Bid Life to yield to Time,
I still behold her radiant glow,
Her tender touch sublime.

"Oh, Heavens Do Forgive My Wrath"

In vain have I waited for the horizon to open
And swallow the violent motion
Of curse and pain the faceless men
Endured in their faithful devotion.
Devotion to God, devotion to man
Devotion to Nature's mandate,
While not allowed to think or pen
Subdued by forces of fate.
Devotion to God they lovingly chose
To worship and dearly love,
Even in times when in disguise so close
Death made a final move.
They wept and hoped their prayers have reached
The ears of their loving Divine,
Though with last breath they humbly beseeched
Their voice struck an empty shrine.
No solace came from the heavens above
No tear shed into the ground,
No grief for the abandoned dove
His clipped wings on the mound.
Betrayed by the world, abandoned by God
Their humble prayers dispelled,
Left at the barren grave-strewn road
Their souls to wander impelled.

Oh, heavens do forgive my wrath
My pain has grown me weary,
The shadows of untimely deaths
Within my breast I carry.
I weep for children from us departed
Young lives withered in dust,
I weep for the pain and grief imparted
Upon their senses thrust.
Two thousand years of guilt unfounded
Two thousand years of carrying
A burden into our existence branded
My ache has made more searing.
Sages of old in their wisdom did

Never envision the thrust
When mankind at their Passions' bid
Destruction turned to lust.
The sages gone, the wisdom blown
The world still makes its mark
Upon the graves through nations sown
From minds of ages dark.

"Oh, Ease My Fear"

Oh, ease my fear of a pointed spear
When eyes of my mind no peace can find.
When remembrances bear, draw a sorrowful tear
And pictures unwind of a world so unkind.

Of the sight of a cry in a helpless child's eye.
Who torn away at his mother's dismay,
With no strength to defy was fated to die,
By a bullet stray from man's moral decay.

Of the glory that shone on the Butcher of Lyon,
When the voices of might broke your will to fight.
When the heart heard the moan 'neath the lonely grave stone,
And the darkness of night turned to horror of light.

Of the madness which fought every kindness of thought,
When terror forbade crowded lines to fade
Of shadows caught in a madman's onslaught,
In an insidious trade to the Satan made.

Of prisons gray, void of sun-warming ray,
Where the bloodthirsty reign of terror and pain,
And the fear-laden day has withered away
With the last remain of a thought's lost train.

Of plundering bands with greedy hands
Tearing through lines of lore wealthy mines
In forlorn lands, abandoned to fiends,
With empty shrines among thorn bearing vines.

Oh, ease my fear, bid the world to hear
The lamenting voice of prayer's lost choice.
With passion and care break the yoke we bear,
The deafening noise of memory's voice.

"Remembrances"

In the solitude of my abode
I reminisce of when I strode
On silent nights and lonely days
Searching for faces, their shadowy ways.
The storm of ages beating upon
The tide of memories etched in stone
Of those departed pale and wan
Faces I will never see again.

Above the clouds in dense smoke written
A lonely tune by anguish smitten
Resounds a broken soul's dismay
Pursued by voice of haunted prey.
The night is deep, I only can
Discern the lion's treacherous den
Where torn wings of fading dreams
The memories and passion screams,
The utterly delusive hopes,
Lie stranded among fraying ropes.

Like tear drops fall the words from skies
Along with muted by wind lies;
Broken branches' creaking cry
Echoes and burning tears lay dry.

Tear not my aching heart away
From all I loved and lost, the day
I left to search for life elsewhere
While Death would not allow to spare
A soul, but with a vengeance swept
The guiltless pray, while my eyes wept.
A stranger to my own disguise
I fled the grip of a cruel demise.

How do I live, survive in the wild
Away from life with surroundings so mild?
How do I live when my heart bleeds and cries
In a world infested with deceptive lies?
With my mind overcast and my head reeling
No one to mend my dismal feeling,
The shadows, a ghostly remainder of past,

Would never depart from my exiled nest.

I saw wisdom fail and compassion die,
I saw deadly fear of vile betrayal cry
When the day of freedom from fetters arose
Only to die without purpose or cause.

"Sing Me, Oh, Sing a Lullaby"

Sing me, oh, sing a lullaby
Let childhood voices reach the sky.
Fifty-one years have past away
Since the gray darkness closed the day
Amid wandering shadows.

The heavy throbbing in my breast,
My wounded heart won't let me rest,
For I can hear and I can see
The muted swallows on the tree
With palsied wings.

The autumn past, the leaves have fallen
Bring back my youth in blooming stolen;
It is my soul's wild fear and pain
Tearing through all my veins again
Like waves of a rising sea.

Wake me; ah, wake from broken dreams
To sunshine's golden, warming beams,
To Life's enchanting fairy tale
To land of rivers, leas, and dales
Where I have left my past.

Your voice will rise, the silence break,
On silver wings the past awake.
My thoughts will bring those gentle years,
Moments the lovely May day wears
Back to my memory.

The crimson rose, the morning dews,
The rays the glorious sunshine strews,
The moon, the cooling midnight air,
The thoughts my idle dreams not dare
Will ease my yearnings.

The murmur of the foaming sea
Will carry childhood's endless glee.
The voices of the past long gone
Will bounce off from the lifeless stone
Like a distant symphony.

A symphony of Passion's strife
To bring my childhood's dream to life.
Longings from a long lost world
Into a deathly exile hurled.
Sing me, oh, sing a lullaby.

"The Mask"

I lived among my enemies
Behind a mask I bought by chance,
One of a few left remedies
To ward off death, it's dreadful glance.

Behind it I have put my true
Pale face I dared not show,
Lest my true nature gives a clue
To my ancestral flaw.

I hid behind it all lost dreams
My youthful mind could spin-
No one should hear my inward screams
Or see my trembling chin.

No one shall ever see that tears
Flowing deep down my heart,
Blinding my eyes in mortal fear,
Make soul from life depart.

My mask lived in a strange new world
Treaded unaccustomed roads
Where man devoid of feelings, cold,
No mercy shared with gods.

It saw the sun shining bright
Above birds singing high,
But when the dark spell covered night
Could not endure the lie.

Oh, cruel fate, oh, destiny!
What evil have I done?
To have my true identity
From my torn body gone.

Around my soul a wall to grow
Someone's cold heart to beat-
Decline my love of life to glow
Bring senses to retreat.

Where are the songs I sang so free?
They're drowned in shadows' screams,
All vanished in the stormy sea
Of devil's pleasure dreams.

And when I stood at freedom's door,
All hopes and feelings wrought
Behind my mask, have crumbled. for
I have cradled a dead thought.

"World War II"

I

Tell me again just how the world
This wicked force obeyed,
Young David asked, his body curled,
His head to one side swayed.
Tell me again how the Germans tore
The brave hearts from your midst,
Waging a terrifying war,
Rending your earth to bits.
I cannot rightly understand
Where were all the braves?
And their duty to defend
Their countries to their graves.

Old Daniel first just shook his head,
Gray hair disarrayed,
And then, his eyes by deep thought led,
Young David's words obeyed
The world did not sit idly, dear,
We fought them tooth and nail,
Five bloody years it took us near,
To tip the victory scale.

Just how it all begun and ended
I do remember well,
But how the world its wounds has mended
For you will be to tell.

It started all when Chamberlain
For sake of Europe's peace,
Gave Czech's and Poland's west terrains,
Wild Hitler's rage to cease.
Now Hitler's appetite has grown,
Just warfare could it sate.
The fear and dread his men have strewn
No power could abate.
The dreadful images in his passion
Inflamed his soul to hate,
To choke the nations with repression,

Erase the human slate.
Abased and loathed great, gallant men,
Enslaved to his commands,
In terrorizing ways were driven
From their own native lands.
His craving never did abate,
Though countries laid to waste,
Compelled his appetite to sate,
Last breath lost in his haste.

One day the evening stars shone bright,
The moon stared at the earth,
But in the distance lie the sight
Of storming, heaving curse.
There black clouds gathered hovering
In heavy presage signs,
And threatening lightning, thundering
Raced in a blinding line.
It was not heaven's angry show,
Nor quivering of earth crust,
God's raging ire could not slow
The devil's forward thrust.
A psychopath's hatred spell,
A maniac's hissing voice,
A vengeance bursting from a shell,
A monster's wicked choice.

It was September thirty-nine
When culmination came,
With 'Blitzkrieg' – Hitler would define –
Begun the bloody game.

There stood the vulnerable host,
All Europe's lost defense,
A feast of glory left to boost
Bloodthirsty Fuhrer's sense.
Hence, his superior race shall rule,
Their mighty fist suppress
All dreaming, freedom loving fools,
Their hopes condemned to death.

And the superior race converged.
Their wings spread land to coast,
Upon the bravest men diverged
From all beleaguered posts.

In months romantic France collapsed,
And Poland in three weeks,
On Holland's, Belgium's, Norway's steps
Now different authorities speak.
The Vichi puppet government
And Quisling of the Norse,
Their patriotic covenant
Assigned to evil force.
Even the British Isles behind
The English Channel waves,
Could not escape the warring grind
Lest they be doomed to slaves.

In Africa the sluggish Moor
Awakened from his sleep
By agonizing canon's roar,
Bewildered stood agape.
The camels, eyes in startling scare,
Abandoned in great haste,
Saw their caretakers unaware
Perish in battle waste.

II
As far as the horizon bow
High conflagration claimed,
Where Russian villages lie low,
Their peasants bodies maimed.
Like Mephistophelean scythe above
Cuts heads condemned to fall,
The Germans crowned with devil's love,
Rejoiced to Fuhrer's call.

And midst the gory horror sprung
The Fuhrer's proudest feats –
Where torture screams, so cruelly rung,

Met deaf ears to entreats.
The concentration camps where death –
Exalted maniac's dream –
Has risen his unabated wrath
To demi-god esteem.
Where life – its passions long suppressed –
With mist and smoke expired,
Its grief and suffering laid to rest,
Its soul from flesh retired.

Two times have seasons passed around
Leaving a ghastly shroud,
The German armies gaining ground
Did eastern soil maraud.
And on the western front raged on
The fiercest battle songs,
Life's noble strifes abandoned, gone
To coarse and vulgar tongues.

It seems like hope has gone forever
With all those years gone by,
And freedom will not come back ever,"
Said David with a sigh.
No, never rested our scorn,
Yet, never left us hope,
Our strength of pain of suffering born
Brought sight to greater scope.
America now has joined its hand
With all oppressed and vowed,
To drive the enemy from the land
Which their ancestors plowed.

Another fall has passed again,
Of leaves stood bared the trees,
The fetid bodies of the slain
Lie chilled on rain soaked leas.
The howling winds came blowing down
From icy northern planes,
Sped rising in a whirling crown
Amidst the blinding rains.

And when the winter's heavy snow
Blanketed the frozen earth.
And Volga's upper water flow
Iced over to the berth,
From Stalingrad's beleaguered port
The Germans fled in dread,
Their Fuhrer's lost abandoned sport,
Their great ambitions dead.

The African sun was shining bright
And shimmered in the air.
The darkness of the passing night
Transformed to freedom's glare.
There General Montgomery
Proclaiming victory,
With shouts of merry revelry,
Has entered Tripoli.
In 'Operation Torch' then Ike –
In one surprise campaign –
His army in one blowing strike
Crushed enemy force amain.

In France confounded German troops,
Heroes of lost intent,
After 'D-Day' crusade – a wretched group,
Their postures downward bent.
Last vestige of a super race,
Their haughty scornful look
Erased from brow without a trace.
Last chapter from a book,
Where mocking lessons taught: no man
Has universal power,
And no amount of fetter can
A freeman bring to cower.
The yoke that tyrants press on wounds
Of proud man's neck will brake
When he – his wrath surpassed the bounds –
His servile posture shakes.

So, every torturing whip shall scream
With ghastly, stark remembrance,
How did one man 's notorious dream
His partisans entrance.
The eyes of memory shall never close,
The voices never drown
In crowded ages to dispose
Of pain to comfort grown.

"The Great Crime"

This is the story why you may regret,
If ever your memory should let you forget,
How nations coerced were made to obey,
By one man's cruel mind, gone astray.
For unless you painfully, carefully heed,
History's lesson may be wasted, indeed.

Still stood the air on dark September,
Etched in the memories of those who remember.
Black clouds suspended, in their breath
Carried forebodings praising death,
And when the world from slumber awoke,
Late was the hour, madness amok.

From high above skies arose a thunder,
Scattering fire down way yonder,
Strewing flames and dust to the east and west,
Echoing deep cries from the mountain crests.
With blazing torches across Europe's plains,
The German armies spread over wide terrains.

Blight and destruction they sowed everywhere,
Encircling free nations trapped in a snare;
Through verdant valleys their armies have trod,
No boundaries, no realms- with no fear of God.
Behind the shadows of this death and destruction,
Stood one maniac's ambitions of world reconstruction.

My tongue the name he has born shall skip,
For fear it may mar and disgrace my lip;
With poisonous wrath his breath infected,
Like fire from a mouth of a dragon ejected.
The man possessed by purity of race,
Jews from this earth has pledged to efface.

While his fist went up in furious gests,
He cried Let 's rid the world of pest
The German people praised his great devise,

They thought it a noble and wise enterprise.
Like demons in black shirts their bodies arrayed,
Haughty, disdainful, dark death they conveyed.

By his side they stood in an endless throng;
Seemingly ordinary people - millions strong -
Yet people who willfully, without warning,
Straight from the altar on a Sunday morning,
With uncontrollable enmity and aggression,
Brutally murdered with a killer's passion.

What fools, so void of sight with blight souls,
As to obey a man so merciless and foul -
Whose one desire, just to please his whim,
Deprived humanity of dignity and esteem;
His mighty crown though threatened by a few -
Yet, threatened by a defenseless, unarmed Jew?

Oh, mockery, oh, travesty of glorious bravery!
To yoke a man and throw him into slavery,
Then, like a devil's monstrous, sinister game,
To feast your eyes upon his misery and shame;
And to his self dug grave to cast the prey,
Whenever your eyes no more avail of play!

Too wearisome the chore for "Herrenfolk" so noble,
The blood, decay - why go through so much trouble?
When with much more proficient skill,
One can bring thousand lives to still.
One knob to tum an odorless and deathly gas,
Would bring their miserable, wretched forms to pass.

There are the chimneys dark and dusty gray.
From which last hopes have fled and smoked away;
Gas chambers with hermetically closed doors,
And human ashes strewn upon the floors.
The names unknown, erased, from earth effaced -
And not a sign the graves above to grace.

There are the children innocent of evil scheme,
And mothers brutally torn away from them;
The old, the sages forward bent with age,
The fathers, brothers, sisters cut down with outrage.
A throng of shadows left behind the walls -
A breathless image of six million souls.

Tell me, you sages in this earthly sphere
For cry of justice, or for human care!
What punishment deserves a crime so dire?
Perhaps the doom that quenched their own desire?
To strike the core in their devastation,
As they have pierced the hearts of our nation.

The peace came back and guns were stilled again,
And home returned the battle-worn men.
No monuments, no medals breasts adorn,
Of those who died in life's early morn.
For the six million killed the peace but brought no morrow,
For those remained just weeping hearts and sorrow.

"Supplication"

Where the valley meets the sky,
Where the hungry ravens fly,
There's a red line on the ridge -
Blood is flowing from the bridge.

Blood is flowing all around,
Bodies spread upon the ground.
Souls suspended in the air,
Clad in sunshine's endless glare.

Tum away your branding eye,
I can hear your shadow cry.
I can hear your breathless moan,
Your heart stilled upon a stone.

High above my prayers go,
My tears spent, my eyes aglow,
My voice piercing through the air -
Why, oh why, does no one care?!

Do the oceans drown the screams,
Flows the blood not in your streams?
Do the mountains block the sights,
Stars are gone, where are all lights?

Deaf are ears, all eyes are blind,
All souls gone, gone is the mind.
Empty hearts are made of stone
Or did madness reach the throne?!

Answer me! Oh, still my ire!
Ease my heart from pain so dire.
Plead I heavens but in vain,
How to endure life again?

Stillness hovers all around
Empty skies above the ground,
Empty souls behind the ridge,
Hungry ravens on the bridge.

"Delirious"

I
Here I lay, my dreams ended,
Broken threads of life unmended.
Here with last of breath I plead;
I'm so young - would someone heed!"

Innocent, untouched by sin,
Far from coarse world have I been;
Sheltered from deceit and lies,
Under loving watchful eyes.

Gently Past before my eyes
Spins with melancholy cries.
Like dew drops on brilliant morn,
Crystal tears my cheeks adorn.

Spins the story of my life,
Tangled happiness and strife;
Childish frolics, carefree play,
Books on shelves in disarray.

There's the little prayer house,
Where the young men did espouse
In their lacy, white array,
Fair maidens, pledging to obey.

Where the learning of past ages,
Imbued wisdom of great sages;
And the ghosts of bygone years,
Lurk from creaking wooden stairs.

There's my home, the winding rills,
Clouds above arranged in frills.
Crimson roses on the path,
Kissed by golden sun's caress.

II
The foreboding in the calm,
Praises death with irksome psalm.
Tempest on her torrid wings,
Circles calm with fiery rings.

Crowds stand gathered on the square,
Stillness lingers in the air.
Bodies huddled in embrace,
Children hushed stand dazed in place.

Strained by vigil hearts stand still,
Voices mute, minds stripped of will,
Immured souls are strapped within
Walls of cruelty and sin.

Stamping hoots, trucks are rolling,
Piercing gun shots, bodies falling.
Orders from the high command,
Bloodstained by satanic hand.

III
All is quiet, still again,
Left is one dark crimson stain,
And the lurking apparition
Of the morbid minds rendition.

Pale and wan, all veiled in sorrow,
Mother's face etched in deep furrow,
Her eyes in an endless stare,
Deep in abyss of despair.

Don't cry mother, shed no tear,
Look, above the skies are clear;
Come and lie beside me,
I'll pray the world be free.

Hold my hand, oh, help me up!
Bring this mad, mad world to stop!
Hold the waters in midstream,
End the lurid, gruesome dream!

All is gone, there is no 'morrow,
Eyes are spent of tears of sorrow;
My wings fly spread beyond azure,
Where souls dwell so kind and pure.

Heaven knows not mortal pain,
Nor the earthly vigil's strain;
On the calm of divine bosom,
Torn dreams again blossom.

There's no hatred bending souls,
Into cruel, monstrous ghouls,
Nor obey they by decree,
Of man's contorted effigy.

"The Train of Death"

Death lurked from every corner
When the journey began
In the cattle train wagons
Where the railroad tracks ran.
Disguised from intended form
His glory days he ruled
In a high ranking uniform
Or as a raging fool.
In a palm of a skilled hand
His presence unbound,
Or as a beguiling friend
On a hostile ground.
He sprang from minds
Of sly, twisted brains
Of tyrants aligned
Along the ill-fated train.

The train moved along
Through snow covered meadows,
With an ill boding song
Death courted the shadows
Of human forms moving
Among descending gloom,
His cunning breath wooing
The curse filled doom.
In the hum of the engine
His puffing breath bred
Like a mischievous urchin
A hard, jeering dread.

Hush, hush frozen meadows
Keep secret the ruse
From ghastly, pale shadows
Their destiny's truth.
I am the master of evil
I live in the minds
Of the ill boding devils.
My breath sweeps and winds
The stormy outbreaks
Of the mighty Fury

Who shatters the weak
Makes life from flash scurry
This good fortune I share
With devils- my team.
It's my pledge not to spare
But consume what they deem
A vermin, pest in one combined
With a dangerous intent
In their sly, wretched mind.
My blood thirsty team
With rapture devours
Their eyes agleam
Those pleasure filled hours.
When their eyes behold
Those hell destines slaves,
Their fate untold
Their last beds- the graves.

The train puffed and blew
The smoke filled breath,
Crossed the cold plains below
Into the roam of death.
It came to a halt
From a slow moving pace
Where iron gate bolts
Screeched in its base.
Where chimneys gray
Toward the azure sky
Spew the smoke, and rays
Of lost sunshine dye.

The days are done
For you poor shadows, lost
In the dull, listless drone
Of the vanishing ghost.
The years will pass
A few will remain
To delete from the grass
The red, searing stain.

Acknowledgements

Revisiting the Holocaust is not an easy task. In my journey to write this memoir, I relied on the feedback of friends and family, most of whom had lost family in the Holocaust. My husband, whose father survived the Kovno Ghetto and Dachau, has been the technical wizard of my book. The feedback from I got from the following people was immeasurable: my sisters Susan Lane and Phyllis Benson, my daughter Dannah Raz Kanaan, niece Jessy Lane, nephew Lee Benson, cousins Gina Friedlander, Irv Geslewitz, Helen Singer Katz, Geoff Zynger and Ronn Friedlander, friends Susan Wildman, Maty Bar and Sheryl Bronkesh.

A special thank you to the Maia Sutnik and Tracy Mallon-Jensen of the Art Gallery of Ontario for their permission to use the photograph of my father for the cover of the book. My deepest admiration goes out to Henryk and Stephania Ross and the other unnamed Jews who risked their lives to help Ross photograph the true conditions of the Lodz Ghetto.

About the Author

Mirla Geclewicz Raz is the daughter of Holocaust survivors. She is on the Board of Directors for the Phoenix Holocaust Association and the head of its Education Committee. In addition to The Birds Sang Eulogies, Ms. Raz is a retired speech pathologist and the author of the popular Help Me Talk Right books as well as a contributing author to other books in her field. She has two grown daughters and a granddaughter. She lives with her husband in Scottsdale, AZ.

You can connect with Ms. Raz at mirlag@speechbooks.com
Visit our web site at http://birdssangeulgies.com

Made in the USA
Middletown, DE
14 September 2021